IT'S EASY T

RAISE AND TRAIN A PUPPY

IN YOUR HOUSE OR APARTMENT

by BOB BECKER

Bob Becker's name is synonymous with the love of dogs and a deep and expert knowledge of the care and training of them. Known from coast to coast for "Chats About Dogs" on the radio, author of several books on raising and training of puppies and grown dogs, recently picked as the "Dog Man of the Year" in the midwest for his outstanding services to dogdom, writer of a syndicated column on dogs, he counsels thousands of owners every year.

GARDEN CITY PUBLISHING CO., INC.
Garden City, N. Y.

To Suzanna, who has eagerly shared the pleasures and joys of dog ownership with me, given freely of her time to the care and education of the canine members of our family down through the years, has borne the anxiety and heartbreaks when they have left us for ever, and has never said "No" when another new dog was added to our canine group!

CONTENTS

Bringing a new puppy from a kennel into the strange surroundings of his new home is a big change for him, so it's wise to give him time to get acquainted. He'll want to inspect everything at first and thus learn about his future home.

Welcoming the New Puppy

So you have a new dog in the home—a cute little puppy! Now the big question is: what are the things you should do for this new member of the family? Is it all right to give the pup a meal? What part of the house should the pup investigate first?

Some of the things which the owner should keep in mind regarding the early treatment of the pup are as follows:

1. If you have bought an eight or ten weeks old dog he won't be housebroken, of course, so you'd better not let him run around in the living room at first. It's much better to turn the little fellow loose in the kitchen. Better cover the linoleum with newspapers.

2. Let him do what he wants to when you first bring him in the house. For example, let him walk around the room and sniff and smell everything. Don't forget that he's in a strange new world. You've taken him from his home and his family, put him in an automobile (perhaps), and then introduced him to a room that has many strange things in it from floor covering to chairs. A little puppy has to have time to figure out this experience.

3. Don't feed the little fellow as soon as you get him home. You might try him on a drink of water, but hold the food until he's less excited. If the pup was transported by automobile he probably was quite frightened by the ride. To give him food at this stage is not advisable.

4. The children naturally will want to fondle and play with the pup as soon as he's in the house. Explain to them that their new pal ought to have a little time to calm down. It's a good idea, also, to tell them to be careful that he does not get banged by a door. And no inexperienced little dog should be forced to walk up or down stairs. Such experiences may scare the pup out of his wits.

1

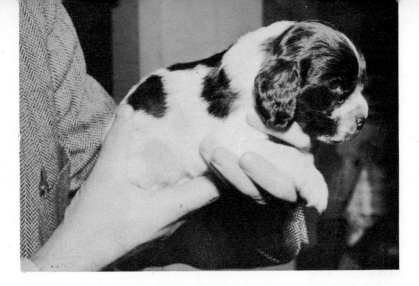

No puppy or adult dog should be lifted by the scruff of his neck. Here's the correct way to lift and carry a puppy, with support under his hindquarters and breast.

5. Don't let the children put a leash and collar or harness on the pup and take him for a walk right away. He has to get used to a leash and collar gradually and that comes later in life when he has confidence in you and his new home.

6. Even though the dog has a kennel odor in his coat, a bath is not advisable. No eight or ten weeks old dog should be bathed, no matter what the season is. You can clean the pup later (if he needs a cleaning) with a brush and a little special cleaning liquid made especially for dogs. These cleaners may be obtained in any store or shop selling pet supplies.

7. The pup may whine the first night or two. That's to be expected because he's lonesome. He'll get over it.

8. The new pet will be less trouble if you have a box bed for him. You can make one out of a large box (if the pup is of a rather small breed). Put a piece of carpet or other soft bedding on the bottom. Shredded newspapers also are good. You can buy some excellent dog beds in pet shops. Confining the dog to a restricted area at night is wise until he's house-broken. Remember he's just an inexperienced little puppy who never had any rules on house manners in the kennel. So don't forget to put newspapers all around his bed and keep them there until he learns something about manners.

Correct Feeding is Very Important

Undoubtedly the most important factor in the health of your dog is its diet. Common sense dictates that meat of some kind be included in your pet's food program in-as-much as dogs are carnivorous animals. Even a pup that's just weaned is fed a little meat. All dogs relish and thrive on a diet containing a certain amount of fresh or cooked horse meat, beef (cheapest cuts, kidneys, hearts, etc.), and mutton. Well cooked pork also is all right. Included in the meat list is a high quality canned dog food. A dry dog food of some type is recommended. When such a food is mixed with meat, the dog has a good ration. Canned fish is another good food for dogs.

Owners should remember that puppies vary greatly in their capacity for food. Even pups of the same breed and litter may not eat the same amounts of food, nor do they require the same amounts of food for adequate growth. If the puppy does not finish some of his meals cut down on the amounts you are giving him.

SUGGESTED FEEDING FOR MEDIUM SIZE, SIX TO NINE WEEKS OLD PUPPIES

8 A.M.—Four to six tablespoonfuls of whole cow's milk or irradiated canned milk (diluted half and half with water), plus a few softened kibbled biscuits, or a heaping tablespoonful of moistened puppy meal. A puppy meal is a dry, granular type of dog food, which you can get in any dog or pet shop and most food stores. A good one contains several kinds of cereals, calcium, vitamins, meat and other nourishing ingredients. All of these meal-type foods must be moistened with milk, warm broth or water. Add two or three tablespoons of cooked or raw ground horse meat, beef or mutton.

Noon—Approximately the same feeding except that you may substitute a little canned dog food for the ground meat. At this time or later in the day add a half teaspoonful of cod liver oil to the pup's meal.

4 P.M.—Mix several tablespoonfuls of moistened puppy meal with a couple of tablespoonfuls of ground and slightly cooked horsemeat, beef or mutton, and a little tomato juice, or cooked tomatoes. Tomatoes agree with most dogs. So do several other kinds of cooked vegetables. But do not give a pup or grown dog large amounts of vegetables. They are strictly subsidiary foods. A dog is not a vegetarian.

Late Evening—Milk. The amount depends on the size of the three previous meals and the capacity of your pup. Try him on a cupful. If he drinks it, okay. If he wants a little more, give it to him. Milk is splendid food for a young pup.

The above amounts are average for a dog of the size of the cocker spaniel, fox terrier, Scotty and other breeds of similar size. You will have to use your own judgment on amounts of the various foods. Obviously if you are over-feeding, the pup will not eat all of his meal.

MEALS FOR A TOY DOG PUP

Small (toy) breeds like the Pekingese, Pomeranian, Chihuahua, toy Manchester and others of that general size require less food than the cocker, Scotty and other breeds for which the above feeding schedule is intended.

But the basic foods are the same. Many dog owners think that different breeds of dogs require radically different kinds of foods. That is not true. The amounts vary according to the size and weight of the dog, but the same horse meat, beef, mutton, lamb, canned dog food, cod liver oil, milk and dry prepared foods that nourish a Scottish terrier also will take care of a St. Bernard or boxer.

8 A.M.—Give the pup several tablespoonfuls of fresh or canned milk.

Noon—Two large teaspoonfuls of slightly cooked ground horse meat or beef. If the puppy prefers the meat raw, that's all right.

4

Late Afternoon—Moisten a tablespoonful of puppy meal with a little warm milk and give it to the puppy.

8:00 or 9:00 P.M.—One tablespoonful of slightly cooked ground horse meat, beef or mutton, with a little moistened puppy meal. Add a quarter to a half teaspoonful of cod liver oil to this or one of the other meals.

Some toy dog breeders believe that Pablum should take the place of ground meat in one meal per day. This feeding consists of one teaspoonful of Pablum plus milk. Others believe a soft boiled egg should be fed at least every other day. Pablum, soft boiled eggs, thick meat soups made with meat, vegetables and a little puppy meal are nourishing for any pup of any breed, if you want to feed these items.

MEALS FOR LARGE BREEDS

If you are raising a collie, German shepherd, setter, boxer, Doberman, pointer, or other breed of that general size, you will have to feed the puppy larger amounts of food. But the basic foods are the same. Sample meals for a collie pup or other puppy in this size group will be as follows:

Early Morning—About a cup of milk plus some kibbled biscuits or meal type of dry dog food. The prepared foods should be moistened.

Noon—A handful of ground beef, horse meat, lamb, mutton, or high grade canned dog food.

Late Afternoon—A tablespoonful of cooked vegetables (tomatoes are good), a cup of ground beef or horsemeat (slightly cooked or raw), and a small amount of puppy meal or moistened kibbles.

Evening—One or two cups of milk with a soft boiled egg. If the pup will drink three cups of milk at night, give that amount to him. The dog also should have one teaspoonful of cod liver oil every day. This can be mixed with his food.

In feeding young, growing and very active puppies the owner should remember this: vary the amounts of food (if necessary) so that the puppy is kept plump. Also, remember that some pups need more than the average amounts, while others remain plump and healthy with slightly less.

MEALS FOR VERY LARGE BREEDS

A St. Bernard, Newfoundland, Great Dane or pup of any other very large breed, gets the same general foods given a Scottish or fox terrier, but in larger quantities. All the large breeds have to be fed plenty of bone building foods (they need lots of calcium), and also increased quantities of dry dog foods. Some breeders advise five meals per day for such pups with just about all the milk they will drink. A great Dane, when eight weeks old, should have five meals per day.

A Great Dane pup at eight or ten weeks of age can eat between a quarter and a half pound of ground horse meat at one meal plus a little dry prepared food. Cod liver oil, ground meats, canned dog foods, lots of milk, and dry dog foods plus coddled eggs are a must in the diet.

MEALS FOR THREE MONTHS OLD PUPPIES

As a rule, kennels give three months old puppies three or four meals per day. The fourth meal usually is made up mostly of milk. No owner should forget the importance of milk in the pup's diet. It supplies much needed calcium for the dog's teeth and bones.

At age three or four months the puppy should be given the same foods as prescribed for it when it is eight or nine weeks old, but naturally in larger quantities. A typical breakfast could be some warm milk poured over a cooked cereal, or warm milk with some kibbled biscuits plus a handful of ground slightly cooked meat, or a handful of canned dog food. The two other main meals should include meat, dry prepared dog food and possibly a coddled egg. For the late evening snack, milk poured over some type of dry dog food is excellent. The cod liver oil daily ration should be continued.

MEALS FOR PUPS FOUR TO TEN MONTHS OLD

Feed three meals per day. Increase the quantities of solid foods. You can gauge the amounts your puppy needs by noting if he eats all the food you give him, and if he is thin, plump or too fat. At this age the pup's diet should have a large percentage of solid foods. The dog should continue to get such basic foods as ground beef, mutton, or horse meat, a horse meat stew with a few vegetables and dry dog food added to thicken it, a high grade canned dog food, an occasional meal of boned fish, dry dog food of some type and cod liver oil. The pup will welcome an occasional smooth bone to chew on.

FEEDING ADULT DOGS

Many experienced dog owners and breeders give their grown dogs a light meal in the morning and the main meal in the evening. Some kennels feed just one meal per day—in the late afternoon. The morning meal may be just a few dog biscuits, a piece of whole wheat toast or some left over cooked breakfast food.

The evening meal can be varied from day to day with dry dog foods, meat of some kind and canned dog food as the mainstays of the diet. Here are some sample meals for the adult dog:

1. Slightly cooked ground horse meat to which kibble biscuits, a hard crunchy type of dog food, meal or other dry foods is added so that the mixture is NOT sloppy. If you want to add some cooked tomatoes (left overs) to this mixture, all right. This is the standard meal for our dogs and they thrive on it. However, we add a little fat to the horse meat which is very lean. All dogs require some fat in their diets. So don't trim all the fat from bones or left over meats. Remember your dog needs some fat to be healthy.

2. High quality canned dog food, either with or without a few cooked vegetables, plus some type of dry prepared food.

3. If your dog likes his meat raw occasionally, feed him some plus a moistened dry dog food.

4. If you have a few meat scraps from a roast (lamb or beef or pork) moisten some dry dog food and add the meat to it.

5. Boned fish plus dry dog food makes a good meal for a grown dog.

Don't be surprised if your pet loses his appetite during very hot weather. Most dogs do not exercise very much during extremely hot weather, so naturally they need less food. In fact, it's a good idea to feed less and also later in the day when the temperatures get high.

HOW MUCH TO FEED

Owners commonly ask us how much they should feed their house pets. Experience and observation will give the answer to this question. If your pet is overweight reduce the food amounts and increase the amount of exercise daily. If the pet leaves part of his meal, take it away from him at once and cut down on the next meal. You want a well fed dog with enough meat on him to cover his ribs. But you do not want a very fat dog. Overweight often shortens the pet's life.

Generally speaking, a medium sized dog weighing eighteen or twenty pounds needs around ten to thirteen ounces of solid food per day. However, the same amount of food that will keep a Scotty, for example, in good condition, may make another one overweight. Dogs are much like people when it comes to food. Some people put on too much weight even though they eat sparingly to moderately. Others eat big meals and stay thin.

PREPARED DOG FOODS

Both puppies and grown dogs can be fed high grade prepared dog foods which are the result of modern scientific research. In fact, the back log of the diet of every dog can be one or more of these prepared foods either dry or canned or both. The dry types come in several different forms. Give the dog the ones he likes the best.

GENERAL FEEDING TIPS

1. Milk is a reliable standby for puppies because it contains minerals, proteins, fats and other nourishing ingredients.
2. Don't let anyone convince you that milk causes worms. That's 100 per cent buncombe.
3. Your dog is a carnivorous animal, now accustomed to eating many foods that humans eat. Therefore, your dog

likes meat and thrives on a diet containing meat in some form.

4. Let your dog alone when he's eating. Don't permit the children to worry him during his meal. A dog has a right to demand to be left alone when it's meal time, just as we like to be allowed to eat our dinner without interruption or annoyance.

5. There is danger in feeding chicken (and other sharp) bones to dogs because they may lodge in the throat or puncture the intestines.

6. Your dog will gulp his food instead of chewing it thoroughly. Don't worry about it. Dogs are able to digest chunks of food.

7. Don't give your puppy smoked sausages, candy and other similar rich foods. Pups do a lot better if they stick to simple foods.

8. Don't believe that old dog fable about raw meat making a dog vicious. That's a ridiculous belief. Some dogs thrive on raw meat. Others don't like it and prefer cooked meat.

9. When you change your dog's diet, do it gradually. This procedure is especially desirable when you wish to give the dog a new kind of prepared food.

10. Dogs like to chew on smooth bones. But this practice can be overdone. Pets that chew too many bones will wear out their teeth.

Every dog should be taught to sleep in the same place every night, so providing some sort of bed for him to enjoy will also help the owner in training him to stay off furniture.

Where Will the Puppy Sleep?

It's much more important to establish permanent sleeping quarters for a young dog kept in the home than most owners realize. Providing some sort of bed or "retreat" for the pet helps to keep it off furniture, makes the dog happier because he knows he has a place of his own in the house, and also helps in training the dog to obey commands. Although every owner has the privilege of letting his or her pet sleep on beds, in chairs and on davenports, most of these owners find that in the long run such indulgence leads to trouble. A spoiled dog can present many problems. One way to spoil the pet is to let him have his own way about sleeping where he pleases.

We have found it worthwhile to give our dogs a bed downstairs, when they are not outside in a small kennel. Our terriers had their beds in the butler's pantry. Every night this location enabled us to school these dogs in the "go to bed" command. This lesson taught them that they had to retire to that bed when ordered and, even more important, that they could not bark nor leave their location. This is very important in teaching the pet that you have control over his actions.

We urge all owners to establish a place for the pet away from the general routine of the household so that it can be used to teach the dog that it must not howl or whine when left alone. Put a comfortable bed or pad there (you can find these at most any dog shop) and make the dog stay there and keep quiet for varying periods of time every day. If you don't do this the dog may resent being left alone to such a degree that it will stage a tantrum when you go to a motion picture show, and thus keep the whole neighborhood disturbed.

A neat little bed (especially one with a mattress stuffed with fragrant cedar shavings) is a good idea for the living room. It also helps you train your dog and keep control over it.

11

Housebreaking

As soon as your new puppy comes into the home you have to decide how you want to housebreak it. If you have a yard or can easily take the puppy outdoors the best procedure is to teach the pup to go outside. But when the new dog is being raised in an apartment it's more convenient to train him to use papers in the bathroom, or other corner of the house. When puppies are acquired during the winter (in the northern tier of states) the cold, snowy weather often is a decisive factor in deciding which method shall be used in housebreaking. It's not wise to try to teach a small pup to use the outdoors when there's a chance of it getting chilled. Serious trouble may result from taking a young pup into the snow and subjecting it to near zero temperatures (or lower) several times a day.

The second situation where paperbreaking is advantageous is when the young dog is being raised on the second, third or higher floor of an apartment. Obviously a little pup can't wait to be taken down an elevator or several flights of stairs, hence the newspapers.

Here's the routine for paperbreaking a puppy:

1. Spread about three thicknesses of newspapers on the floor, preferably in a room covered with tile or linoleum.
2. Place the puppy on the paper several times each day and always after a meal. When it does what it is supposed to do praise it lavishly.

Watch the puppy closely when it is in the house. Remember that a very young dog often will not give you much of a signal. If you detect the slightest "danger" signal, rush the pup to its papers and keep it there as long as necessary.

When it misbehaves on the floor or rugs hold it close to the soiled spot and say "No, No" in a low firm tone of voice.

Repeat these words to impress the dog with the fact that you are displeased. Be stern enough to make the dog understand that it has done wrong. But don't whip the little fellow. Too much discipline may cow your pup.

You'll have to watch the pup very closely for the first week or so, so you can praise it when it does what it should do and correct it (with your voice) when it makes a mistake. The biggest mistake that most owners make in teaching house-manners is that they expect a very young pup to think like a human being. After all, an eight or ten weeks old pup fresh from a kennel is just an infant that knows nothing about living with people. You can't expect it to learn something in one or two lessons. Every dog wants to please the owner. But they can't please us unless we show them what we want done and are patient in explaining how they should do it.

Training a dog to go outdoors usually takes a shorter period of time because it is more natural for it to use the ground. The routine is much the same as in paper breaking. The younger the pup the more often it has to be taken outdoors. Give the pup every possible chance to get into the correct routine by taking it outdoors the first thing in the morning, after every meal and once or twice between meals. As it grows older and learns its manners the number of trips to the yard can be reduced.

It will help a great deal if you take the pup to the same spot everytime. This is a case of association of ideas which often speeds up the routine you are trying to establish.

Be sure to praise the puppy when it does as it should. Continue this practice until it is perfect in its house manners.

HOUSEBREAKING HINTS

1. The cardinal rule of housebreaking puppies is to praise them when they behave properly, shame and scold them when they misbehave.

2. Don't be too harsh in disciplining your pup. You "whip" a young dog by taking him by the neck, looking him in the eye, and shaming him for a minute or two. There is no need to take a switch to the very young dog. He'll get the idea of the lesson without a real whipping. It's

very easy to ruin a young sensitive dog by being too harsh with him.

3. If you want to be prepared for an "accident" get one of those products that eliminates dog stains on rugs, if used in time. These preparations are available in most department and pet stores.

4. If the pup has soiled a rug the spot may be a temptation to him. You can avoid this by treating the spot with a liquid which will discourage the pup from going back to it and making another "mistake." This preparation can be obtained in pet shops and department stores.

5. Remember that the younger the puppy the more often you must take it outdoors or put it on its papers.

6. Some puppies learn their house manners quickly; others seem to be slow. Sometimes a dog is naturally slow in learning. More often the owner is at fault when the pup doesn't learn its house manners. Rare is the pup that doesn't want to please its owner and isn't clean in a home.

7. Don't expect a six, seven, or eight weeks old puppy to learn how to behave in the house as quickly as an older dog. Pups of that age are too young to absorb such lessons in a hurry.

This Scottish terrier pup is getting his lesson in house manners by being placed on papers several times each day.

Early Leash and Collar Training

Every young dog must be taught that there are times when it must wear a collar and be controlled by it and a leash. In fact, a leash and collar are required accessories when you take your dog for a walk, and also during all the training lessons you give your pet in order to get control over it and teach it good manners. Therefore the pup has to be introduced to a leash and collar fairly early in his life.

Before the pup is old enough to be taken outdoors for walks by all means give him some indoor lessons on the use of a collar. The point is that many young dogs are very much frightened if you just snap on a collar and leash and then hustle them outdoors for a stroll. Use a narrow collar or light chain—never a harness for a training outfit. A harness encourages a dog to strain and tug and thus makes it harder to handle. And a harness may injure a puppy during the time he is growing up. By pulling and straining against it, his elbows may turn out and make him appear bowlegged. If you want to decorate your grown, trained dog with a handsome harness, that's up to you. But when you are trying to train your young dog, he should wear a collar and leash.

Here are the steps in training a puppy to leash:

1. Place a small collar on his neck some day when you are playing with him in the house. Let him wear it around for several days to become accustomed to it. Don't let the children take the pup out for a walk five minutes after he has started to wear a collar. They are apt to scare him to death by dragging him over the grass or the sidewalk. Remember a seven, eight or nine weeks old pup is just an infant. He can't learn everything in five minutes.
2. When the puppy is used to the idea of wearing a collar attach a short leash to it and let him drag it around the house. (Don't permit the dog to chew on the leash.)

15

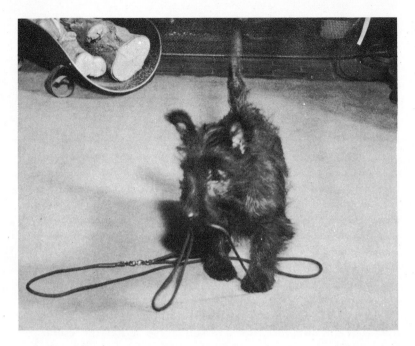

Wearing a collar and leash indoors, This Scottish terrier pup is becoming acquainted with these important accessories which are needed during his early training. Later the puppy will be gently guided by the leash and collar so he won't be afraid of either.

3. By the third or fourth day (or sooner) it's time to take hold of the leash during one of the indoor lessons. Don't be too rough about this at first. Guide him gently by means of the leash for just a few steps, so he will not be frightened by the pressure on his neck. If you are careful about these first lessons and don't frighten the little fellow he'll soon accept the idea of being controlled by pressure from the leash and collar.

4. If the puppy plops down in the house or on the sidewalk in protest against the collar and leash, move ahead and call him to you. Never drag the dog by means of a leash.

By considerate treatment your pup will learn its leash lessons readily. They're very important lessons because later in life the dog must wear a leash and collar when out for a walk and all of his lessons in obedience are conducted with these accessories.

Jumping on People

Lively, demonstrative dogs are a lot of fun. We like to see our dogs register pleasure when we come home after a day at the office. However, there is such a thing as overdoing a welcome by leaping and jumping on you. This can be a very annoying habit and when children are involved, it can be slightly dangerous. A good sized pet may frighten and even knock down children although the dog may have nothing but the friendliest intentions. Then, too, there is the problem of a jumping dog soiling your clothes.

Your young dog can be taught not to jump on you. Older dogs which through carelessness have been allowed to develop the habit can be cured of it if the owner or a trainer gives the offending pet enough lessons.

Because the jumping up business is a habit, you can start your dog on a routine of *not* leaping on you by doing just a few simple things. For example, every time you call your dog to you, just lean over as he gets close to you and give him a pat. Show him you are pleased that he came to you when you called his name and said "Come here." If he's a lively, bouncy and affectionate pup he'll wiggle around and want to play. That's all right at first. The big point in this routine is that you are leaning over to him and *your hands* have been brought to his level.

This gives you a certain amount of control over the dog and without crushing his spirit you can keep him from jumping up on you. If he makes an effort to put his paws on you, firmly but gently take hold of his collar and put him down.

If every member of the family will make a point of leaning over to the dog when he rushes up and get him into the habit of accepting praise and petting with all his feet on the ground, he'll have little desire to jump on you. In other words, a little work will prevent the jumping habit.

A dog that jumps on you or your guests can be a real nuisance, especially when his paws are dirty. This bad habit may be stopped by proper training.

Actually, the smartest thing a dog owner can do in this routine to prevent jumping is to teach the dog (when it's four, five, or six months old) to come to you and sit down and then receive the praise and petting it likes. You can't teach a six weeks old pup such lessons, but when it's a few months old it's ready for them. And it's a very simple but valuable control lesson, too.

Suppose your lovable little dog who looks up to you and likes you very much comes racing to you. This is the time for you to lean over to him when he gets close. He wants the praise that you give him with your hands. Now take hold of his collar with your right hand, lift that hand slightly and at the same time press on his flanks with your left. As you do this say, "Sit, sit" and down he sits because of the pressure on his flanks. Hold him there a few seconds and then let him get up. Tell him "good dog" and praise him.

If this routine is repeated every time the pup comes to you, he'll soon get into the habit of sitting down in front of you because he knows that he's going to be praised to the skies for so doing. He also knows that it won't be only praise by voice. Your hands are going to be on him as soon as he sits. That's what he wants.

Dogs that have been allowed to become offensive jumpers can be corrected in several ways. For example, one nationally known professional trainer suggests that you seize the jumping dog's front paws and then make the animal walk backward for several yards. This is not a pleasant experience for a pet, especially when the owner is scolding it during the exercise.

Another system is to catch the front paws of the jumper and as you scold him you step on the toes of a back foot. Before long the pet will realize that everytime he jumps up on you something decidedly unpleasant happens to him. Naturally every member of the family must cooperate in these training lessons. And everyone should be careful about carrying out this corrective lesson in order not to injure the pet.

Staying Alone Without Howling

A large percentage of owners of pet or companion dogs can hardly wait until their puppies are old enough to learn tricks. Much time often is spent on these cute dogs to teach them all kinds of amusing routines. If we had our way there would be a law against teaching pet canines to speak, sit up, or do any trick until owners had taught their dogs to stay alone and keep quiet. If owners only knew how important the "stay alone and like it" lesson was, they'd buckle down to this training first and let the trick business wait.

The pet that goes into a tantrum when left alone, and barks and whines until all the neighbors are up in arms, invariably is a product of this routine in the home: the whole family is so devoted to the pet that he has his way most of the time. He's talked to, or played with, whenever anybody in the family has time to give him lots of attention. When it's time to do the shopping, the pup goes along. Practically every minute of the day, the dog is taught to *expect* attention and human company. But nobody takes time to give him lessons in obedience so he will respect a command and learn that he has to defer to authority. And not once is he told to go to his bed or corner and stay by himself for an hour or two. As a rule, the pup is thoroughly spoiled after a few months of this wrong kind of dog care.

Some evening the family goes to the motion picture theatre. The pup is put in the kitchen and told to be a good dog! He proceeds to make as much noise as ten dogs. This is only natural. The family has taught the pet to expect human company all the time. Nobody told this pet that some times he'd have to stay alone and keep quiet. You can't blame the pup for raising a rumpus when left alone. His yapping is a normal reaction to the training the family gave him.

The cure is first a good course in obedience training. The dog must be taught that he can't have his way all the time. He must learn that you are the boss. He must obey your commands without question. The objective of the training is control over your dog.

After this training is under way, establish a bed or retreat for the dog in a room away from everybody. Put the dog there and tell him to "Stay." Now leave him alone. When he yowls or whines, go to him at once, scold him and if necessary take him by the neck and shake him a couple of times.

Do this several times every day. Soon he will learn (if you are consistent with your training and firm with the pet) to keep quiet. Now you must test him on his behavior when you leave the house. Put the dog on his bed. Tell him to keep quiet. Make believe you are leaving the house. Slam the door. Then keep quiet. The chances are that he will believe you are gone and then he'll start howling.

Now you really must be stern. No fooling this time. Rush to the dog as quickly as you can. Break in on one of his "solos" and take hold of him. Scold him for a minute or two. Make him understand that you are very angry. Bear down on him so he won't forget the lesson. Put him back on his bed and leave him there for a long time.

Repeat this lesson several times. If you are firm and have control of your dog by means of obedience training, he'll learn to stay alone and not howl.

If this training is not given to a dog, the alternative is a "dog sitter" isn't it?

The big point, we repeat, in this problem of quieting the howling dog is obedience. The spoiled, untrained dogs make the best howlers. There is no way to cure them except by training. We know of just three alternatives to an obedience training routine. First, use of a muzzle, which we consider cruel. And it's unnecessary if the owner is on the job. The second is hiring a dog sitter to stay with the dog! That's unnecessary if the owner trains his pet the right way. The third is getting rid of the dog which is a terrible choice when you love a dog so much.

Correcting the Chewing Habit

Practically every puppy has the desire to chew things in the house or in a small kennel. The average small pup not only will try his milk teeth on pieces of wood, electric light cords, shoes and bones, but often swallows inedible objects. The reason is: a young pup hasn't much sense! Anyway, they are great "samplers" and will try anything once.

Another reason for the chewing habit in pups is that the pressure of rather hard objects against their milk teeth and gums when they are teething feels good. Every pup usually sheds its first set of teeth around the 4th or 5th month. That's the time when chewing exercises feel mighty good, so it's a good idea to give the dog a smooth bone or a hard biscuit so he can work on them.

Inasmuch as nearly every young dog likes to chew objects of most any size or "flavor," don't expose him to temptation. Don't leave him in a room where he can damage household articles when you are not watching him. The easiest way to correct the chewing habit is to prevent it before it starts. So never give the small pup with a desire to sample anything opportunities to use his teeth.

The second training routine is to provide several hard objects for the young dog so he can use his teeth on them any time he wants. If the pup starts to work on an object that is taboo, take him by the scruff of his neck and talk to him as you use the reprimand "No-o-o." Then hand him a hard rubber bone, a smooth natural bone or other similar object that he must learn is his.

At first we can't expect any happy go lucky pup to distinguish between a shoe, slipper or other valuable item in the home that he should not touch, and something that's on the approved chewing list. That's doing the pup an injustice. A dog is a dog and doesn't think like a human being. Anyway, an 8 weeks old puppy fresh from the kennel can't be expected to do much thinking or reasoning.

WATCH THAT PUPPY!

If the pup gets out of hand on this tendency to chew things because you have not been vigilant enough you may resort to the use of repellents.

For example, a little pepper on the sole of a shoe or rubbed on a table leg that the pet has been attacking, will soon discourage the chewing habit. Quinine and pepper applied to objects that the dog likes to chew also will take care of the problem. Or visit the shop where you get pet supplies and obtain a preparation that is made to keep dogs from using their teeth on objects. It has a vile taste but won't hurt a dog.

Repellents are the *last* resort in correcting the chewing habit. We never have used them except in experiments to see what kind and how much of a repellant will stop a dog from chewing an object. If you are bringing up your dog with firmness, kindness and patience he will learn that he can't put his teeth into everything in a room. If you neglect the pup's training it is more than likely he may get into a chewing routine.

The obedient dog, the one that looks up to its owner and responds to the owner's commands, is 100 times easier to handle when it starts to chew objects than the one that is allowed to do what it pleases. Older dogs that try to wreck a room when left alone are invariably spoiled, untrained, disobedient pets. They attack objects with their teeth out of pure spite. They're mad because they have been left alone and you can't blame them for getting mad. They weren't trained to stay by themselves and behave.

If your dog is age 6 months, 1 year, or 5 years and you can't trust him anywhere because he will chew things, you have only one course to follow: start teaching the pet obedience and get control over him. Make him mind when you speak to him. Put him through obedience exercises at least twice each day and see that he obeys a command when given just *once*, not after it's repeated two or three times.

"No, shame on you," is the correct scolding for a dog that insists on using a soft chair for sleeping purposes.

Keeping the Dog Off Furniture

If you do not want your lovable little dog to take catnaps on your nicest chairs or on the davenport you'll have to keep these training points in mind:

1. Never take the young dog in your arms and then sit down in a chair to hold him for a while. That's an excellent way to teach the little fellow that he can get into a chair any time he wants because you were the one that first put him on furniture. It's not right nor is it sensible to try to train a dog to stay out of chairs when you are *not* in the room, if you encourage him to sit with you on a chair some time during the day.

2. Don't leave the new dog in a room at night where he can use a chair for a bed. That's encouraging him to make use of furniture. All dogs like a good bed. Most of them are smart enough to pick a good soft one. You can't blame a pet for picking a cushioned chair in preference to the floor when it comes time to curl up for a nap. That just shows they are smart and the owner must be equally smart in training the pet to use his own bed for sleeping or loafing purposes.

3. If your pup persists in getting on the davenport or sleeping in a chair, be firm with him. Take him by the scruff of his neck, give him a little shake and scold him. Then put him on his own bed. If this doesn't work you can discourage him further by getting a repellant powder at a dog shop and sprinkling a little of it on the chair or other piece of furniture that the animal likes to use.

4. In all of this teaching the big point to remember is that the untrained dog, the disobedient one, will be much more difficult to handle than the pet given obedience training. If your young dog is getting daily obedience lessons so it will recognize you as the boss, it will be comparatively easy to teach it not to sleep on chairs. The spoiled, disobedient dog that has its way most of the time, will resent the furniture training and be much harder to handle.

Teaching the Meaning of "No"

There are few if any words that you can put in the dog's vocabulary that exert more control than a sharp, snappy "No." We consider it the most important single word to be taught the young dog that is trying to learn its place in the family circle. In housebreaking your new pup "No" is a must which also carries with it reproof. If you use it with a low displeased tone of voice, your dog will know that he has done something wrong, or is about to violate some rule of conduct.

For example, in housebreaking a pup you hold him close to the spot he has soiled and say "No-o-o-o . . . No-o-o-o . . . sha-a-me on you." When you find him working on a shoe or slipper you take it away from him as you say "No-o-o . . . No-o-o," keep repeating the word as you hold the shoe in front of him, and then hand him one of his rubber toys or a smooth bone. If the pup whines and howls in his kennel or when he is confined to his bed you snap that word "No!" at him.

In these early training routines the dog quickly learns that the word indicates you are very angry with him and whatever he is doing must be stopped at once. So use "No" in any situation in which the dog is misbehaving. Suppose you put the dog on a rug outside of the dining room and tell him to stay there. If he's smart he'll try to fudge on the command and slowly sneak into the room. And if you are smart about dog training you'll snap that word "No" at him, point to his place on the rug and make him stay where he was ordered to remain.

It won't do a bit of good to say "No" to your dog when you are correcting it unless you speak in a low tone of voice and make the pup believe you are very mad about the whole situation. If you speak to your pet in a soft "now you be a nice dog" tone, he'll know you don't mean it. But if you get your face close to his when you correct him, and all but growl a "No-o-o" at him and at the same time give him a shaking, he'll learn this important command in a hurry.

Training to Heel

Any owner who wants to be proud of his or her pet and also get the most pleasure in taking the pet for a walk, will devote some time to teaching the heel command. The objective is to teach the dog to walk quietly on your left side without pulling and tugging on the leash.

And how early in the life of the pup can you teach him to heel? Willy Necker, Wheeling, Ill., professional dog trainer and at one time in charge of war dog training for the U.S. Coast Guard, says that he will take an average companion dog at the age of five months or thereabouts. Pups of this age can be taught to heel and obey other simple obedience commands. Six months is better for what he calls this preliminary training in good manners. For advanced training he likes to have dogs around nine or ten months of age. However, some pups can be started on their obedience work (very simple things) at the age of four months.

To train the dog to heel you put the collar and leash on him. Give the dog his lessons in the backyard at first, or in some other quiet place. Put him at your left side. Carry the excess part of the leash in your right hand so you can shorten up on it with the left. Some trainers bring the leash around behind them and hold the end in the right hand.

When you walk with the dog and he tries to rush ahead pull him back until he's at your side and say "Heel." If he stays in that position praise him. Give him a friendly pat. If he lags bring him up into position so that his shoulder is at your left knee, and again repeat the command. Then slacken the leash just a little. If he again rushes ahead speak to him sharply and say "Heel" as you pull him into position.

Repeat this routine several times a day. When you have your dog pretty well under control so that he walks at your left side without pulling on the leash, continue this training on the street. But at the start it's advisable to conduct these lessons where the pet cannot be distracted by people, cars and other dogs.

WALKING OR HEELING OFF LEASH

Graduation exercises for the house pet taught to walk like a gentleman on a leash is to stay at heel without a leash on his collar. This is the objective you are working for . . . to have your pet so completely under control and so obedient that he will stay at your left side without being compelled to do so by a collar and leash.

Rehearse your dog in this exercise only when you have given him enough lessons with a leash. At first conduct your lessons without a leash away from any distractions. Don't take him on the street during those first days that you are controlling him by voice instead of the leash. When you feel sure of him, give him a test on a street where he may be tempted to leave your side. If he leaves you or has a tendency to get ahead of you while off leash, snap it on again and continue the lessons with his collar and lead.

Every well trained dog must display his obedience by walking off leash. And most any dog in the world today can learn to do it, from a little Yorkshire terrier to a burly St. Bernard.

This cocker walks like a little gentleman because he's been taught the command to "heel."

Teaching the Dog to Sit

Every well behaved dog should sit down on command, for it gives the owner control over the pet. This is one of the easiest commands to teach. First you put a collar and leash on your dog. If it's a good sized breed you get a short grip on the leash with your right hand so you can pull the dog's head *up*. With the left you press down on his flanks as you snap the command "Sit."

The combination of pulling the dog's head and body slightly upward and the down pressure on his rear will put him in the sit position. Keep repeating the command "Sit" as you force him to sit next to you. Keep him down for a moment or two. If he tries to wiggle around and do anything but sit, increase the pressure of your hand so he has to keep the sitting position.

If you own a small breed you can just take hold of his collar instead of seizing the leash a few inches from the collar. But the safest and easiest way to get that upward movement of the dog's head and body is to use the leash to exert pressure on the animal's neck and body.

If the dog wants to play, use the leash to put him in position; don't coax him to do what you want him to do. Make your commands snap. Handle the dog with authority so he knows that it's not playtime.

As soon as the dog has learned to sit promptly you are ready to take him into the next lesson which teaches him to sit and then stay until you give him the release order.

The "Sit" command is important in every house pet's training. Here is the first position in teaching it - - one hand on the dog's flanks, other hand holding leash to keep the dog's head up and steady.

At the command "Sit" you press down on dog's flanks so he has to sit. Both leash and collar should be used during the lesson. At first you may have to keep him sitting by pressure as hears the command "Sit" repeated.

The "Stay" Command

This is an invaluable word for every dog to know. We use it a dozen times a day in our home. Again, here is a command that makes for good manners in every dog and gives the owner the authority to make a pet behave. And it's very easy to teach a pet. You start on the "Stay" command after the dog has learned to sit. Put on his collar and leash. Have him take the sit position. Now back away from the pet while holding the leash in your left hand, lift your right, palm toward him, and snap the command "Stay." That means the dog must remain sitting down until he gets a release.

If the dog gets up and comes to you, pull him up rather sharply with the leash as you say "No," take him back to the spot where he was told to sit, make him sit down and again back away from him as you say "Stay."

Keep him sitting for a minute or two as you hold on to the leash. Then you can call him to you and praise him for doing as he was told.

The next step is to back away from him as he sits in front of you and stays on command, and (while holding the leash) walk around him. Walk around him one way. Then reverse and go around him the other way. Keep giving him the "Stay" command and hold up your hand to remind him that not only the voice but the hand signal indicates he must not move.

After several lessons like this you can drop the leash and go through the above routine. But be ready to take hold of the leash if the dog tries to fudge on his commands. Be quick to correct him and above all be firm.

The final test for the pet in the sit and stay position is to keep increasing the distance between you and the dog. If he is obedient and wants to please you, it's possible to walk 20, 30 or 40 feet from him and he will not leave the sit position until he's told to. At first you'll leave the leash on his collar.

That represents a control accessory and he knows it. But finally you will take off the leash, make him sit, tell him to "Stay" and walk away from him. Try him on this for two or three minutes; finally for five minutes. If you have taught the pet that you are the Boss and must be obeyed completely and without cheating, he'll not move until ordered.

The next step in control is to have a word that tells the dog he can leave the "Stay" position and come to you.

The simplest word is "Come." Just say "Trigger," (or whatever the dog's name may be), "come." Make the command sharp and snappy.

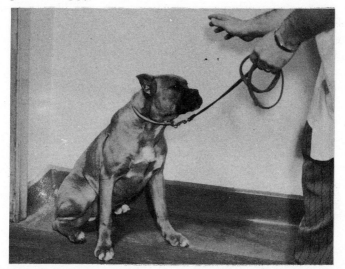

When in the "Sit" position the dog learns the meaning of the command "Stay." Note how this boxer is being taught that the hand extended toward him, palm open, means the same as the spoken command "Stay."

Actually you can use any word you wish for a house pet that isn't going to compete in obedience tests. For one of our terriers, we used the word "Aw-right." This release word was spoken in a rather high tone of voice as compared to the lower tones used to give a command.

Whatever you use to bring the dog to you after it has stayed in one place, be sure and praise him when he reaches your side. Make him understand that you are pleased with his fine behavior.

Teaching the "Down" Command

This command is the same as "Lie down," "Charge" or other similar word that makes the dog lie down. It's an indispensable command in every house pet's education and an absolute must in obedience exercises. Dogs do not like to sit for a long time. It's not a relaxing position for any pet. You'll notice that when you tell your pet to sit and stay, as, for example, at the entrance to the dining room while you are eating a meal, he'll sit if he's obedient and then even without a command slide down to the more comfortable "Down" position. Our Labrador retriever does this nearly every morning when she comes in from her kennel.

To teach your dog the meaning of the word "Down," you first give it the "Sit" command. When the pet is sitting lean over slightly and place your left hand on his shoulders. With the right take hold of his front feet. Now press down with the left (on his shoulders) and at the same time gently but firmly pull his front feet outward. The pet can't help assuming the "Down" position if you do this correctly.

Be sure and let go of his feet when they become horizontal with the ground or floor, but keep your hand on his shoulders. That pressure may be very necessary during the first lessons. Of course, as you pursue this simple routine you give the command, "Down," "Down."

The followup is the same as in teaching a dog to sit. Make the pet stay down until you give him the release word. As the lessons continue and you find him obeying you quite well, move away for several feet after giving him the "Stay" command. In other words, conduct this lesson in the same way as during the "Sit-Stay" routine.

Finally, after more rehearsals of this "Down" and "Stay," you'll take off the dog's leash. Then you will ask the dog to stay down for longer periods as you move farther from him.

The final routine in this entire course of training is to get out of the dog's sight for a minute or two. If he gets up and starts to look for you, take him by the collar and walk him right back to the spot where he should have stayed and put him down again.

Repeat this lesson until the dog is obedient and doesn't get up. Then increase the length of time you stay out of sight. At first the pet may be rather worried about your leaving him. But as soon as he learns that you, the Boss, will come back and praise him he'll stay where he's told to.

Remember that both the "Long sit" and the "Long down" are not only obedience exercises important in competition, but also factors in good manners. Training a dog to mind you so you have control and it has good manners isn't any different from the training for regular obedience tests.

In teaching a dog to lie down you take hold of his front paws and slide them into horizontal position, while pressing down with the other hand so he has to assume the "Down" position.

Training Your Dog to Come

This is one of the most important features of all the training or education you can give to your pet. It leads to control and good manners. In fact, response to the "Come" command may save your dog's life some day on the street.

Of course, the little pup you own gets some preliminary training to come to you when ordered early in the home. You call him by name, maybe clap your hands, and lean over to him as you say "Trigger, come here."

But only by final training outdoors and by getting your pet into the *obedience groove,* will he respond to the "Come" command at any time and under any circumstances.

By obedience groove we mean a state of mind in your pet that never questions your authority.

TEACHING THE COMMAND

You will need a chain collar (you can buy one in any store selling dog accessories) and a long cord or rope to teach the "Come" command. Don't forget that at the start you can give the dog some lessons indoors, especially when he's under five months of age. But by all means finish the course of training *outdoors.* When you take the pup outside in the yard give the first lessons in a spot where he won't be disturbed by other dogs, people coming and going or other distractions. Later, when you have him pretty well under control, you will want temptations to test his obedience so you can correct any slack behavior.

The lesson itself is simple. Tie the cord, which should be forty or fifty feet long, to the pet's collar. Let him get away from you some fifteen or twenty feet and then say "Trigger, come here." Make the command snap. If he doesn't start

"Come" is the command being taught. A cord is being used to make the pet respond to this important command which gives the owner control of a dog outdoors when off a leash.

In teaching pets to come when called, some will respond quickly. Others must be taught that they have to obey whether they like it or not. A long cord on the dog's collar must be used until he has his lesson pretty well learned.

Always praise your dog when you are training him and he does what's he's asked to do. This cocker has "come" on command so is now being told he's a "good dog."

toward you at once, give the cord a little jerk and make him come to you.

Before the dog reaches your feet lean over, take hold of his collar and make him sit down in front of you to the command of "Sit." This is an easy routine to teach as you take hold of the dog's collar with your right hand and pull his body upwards as your left presses down on his flanks to make him sit down. Hold him in that position for a few seconds (at first) and then praise him. Tell him what a good dog he is. Make him understand that you are much pleased with his conduct.

Now you want the pup to get up and move around again. We use the word "All right" for this. We say it in a conversational tone. Even our hunting dogs are sent on ahead by "All right" when we're out walking with them. Or you can send the pup away by "Hie on."

When he's twenty or thirty feet from you and probably sniffing something on the lawn, again call him . "Trigger, come here" and again make it firm and commanding. If he hesitates in coming to you, use the cord and make him come in. This lesson must be given a couple of times each day. Always praise the dog when he responds to the command. Always have your hands ready to show him you like him and are pleased with him.

When the pet comes to you quickly on the command, you may drop the cord to the ground. But keep it close to you so you can pick it up, or step on it if the pup gets a notion to go next door. Let him run around a little and then rehearse him without using the cord.

THE FINAL EXAMINATION

The final test on the "Come" command is to have the dog tempted by something that will take his attention from you and your command and perhaps cause him to want to delay in coming back to you when given the order to "Come." You can arrange for these tests outdoors by having a friend walk by. Or have a dog on leash walked near you and your pet when he's being put through the "come" routine.

If your pupil doesn't do too well in one of these tests go to him, take him by the collar, speak to him sharply, scold him, maybe give him a good shake by taking hold of his neck, and make him come with you to the point from which you were calling him. The idea is to impress on his mind that you are the boss and *must* be listened to.

These "temptation tests" are a regular feature of the training classes for owners now being conducted in many cities and towns from coast to coast. For example, when the class is rehearsing the command whereby the dogs are put down and told to stay until commanded to get up, the trainer will walk around among the dogs clapping his hands to see if the canine pupils can be distracted.

When you are teaching your pet to come to you it isn't absolutely necessary that you make him sit when he has obeyed the command and is in front of you. But getting the pet into the routine of sitting down after coming to you is a wonderful method of *preventing* the happy and very lively dog from jumping on you. It's an additional angle in control and good manners. And those are, in the final analysis, the objectives of all obedience work for the average pet not scheduled to compete in obedience classes.

After hours of patient training with collar and long leash or cord, this cocker is under control so that he comes when commanded without the use of the control. Note how the young trainer extends his hands to encourage the dog.

What to do About the Barker

The dog that barks excessively annoys the owner and often the entire neighborhood. This fault plus the car chasing habit undoubtedly do more to create anti-dog feeling in a community than anything that house pets may do.

Therefore it behooves all of us who own dogs to recognize the fact that unnecessary barking is a fault that we should correct.

One basic point about excessive barkers that all of us must keep in mind is this: in practically every case the owner must take the blame if his or her dog yips from morning until night. You can write off some of the barking as due to the temperament of the dog. There isn't any doubt but what some breeds are more high strung than others. And individual dogs of most any breed may vary in their makeup so much that some want to bark at the slightest provocation, while others have calm, placid dispositions and rarely become nuisances due to too much vocal effort.

But in the final analysis whether your house pet yips too much and at the wrong times, is up to you. In at least 95 out of 100 cases the owner does not get control over the young dog at a time it is developing into a nuisance barker. Then the habit is formed and the dog is almost mature before a start is made to control the barking. That's the wrong way to approach this annoying habit in dogs. You'll find that most nuisance barkers are pretty much spoiled, have their way most of the time, and if they mind at all and listen to a command it's only when the owner is close to them.

The best way to correct excessive barking is to *prevent* it! Let's take a look at how you can raise a pup *not* to bark too much.

The system is extremely simple. All you have to do is train your dog to obey commands and never question your authority! Most young dogs will be inclined to bark when a stranger comes around the house. This watchdog behavior may not develop until the dog is near maturity or it may show up early. That's all right. You want your pet to sound an alarm. You want him to take the responsibility of looking after the home. But don't let him overdo it!

You can keep him from overdoing it by giving him obedience training as soon as he is old enough to absorb it. Make him sit on command, come when called and above all teach him the word "No." That will be your control word in this training to prevent excessive barking.

Suppose the pet starts to bark as a dog rushes through the yard. He has a perfect right to call that dog names in canine language! The dog is trespassing. But don't let the pet rush from one room to another while yipping his head off. Give him that command "No" and speak to him sharply. The idea is that he must understand he has sounded his alarm, you appreciate it, but nix on the vocalizing to excess.

If you have a stubborn pet, one hard to handle, keep a collar and short leash on him during this training. Take hold of the leash and emphasize your command: "No, quiet, no," by giving the leash a sharp jerk so he knows you mean business.

Suppose it's the grocery boy. The dog hears him come up the driveway or approach the kitchen door. He barks. That's all right. He should announce the presence of a stranger with some barking. Now speak to the dog. Talk to him. Tell him that's fine. But give him that "No" or "Quiet" command and make him *sit down*. If he wants to rush around, take hold of that leash and MAKE HIM SIT. Keep him there in position.

Now when the delivery boy comes in it's time for the dog and the visitor to take a minute to get together. You can ask the latter to speak to the dog and pet him a minute or two.

If you keep your pet under control by means of obedience training and a stern attitude when necessary, make the dog mind that command "No" and stop barking when told to, you can keep your pet from becoming a nuisance barker.

TELEPHONE BARKERS

Many owners write us that they are at their wits end because their pets bark so much when the phone or front door bell rings. Most of these harassed owners report that they have whacked their pets many times with folded newspapers but it does no good. And not a few say that the dog is so wild that they can't get hold of him for several minutes to do the whipping.

To these puzzled owners the advice is: throw away the folded newspapers. Stop the whipping. You are just wasting your time and also making the dog more of a problem. The first thing to do is to *train* that pet to obey. Obviously the dog is completely out of hand. It isn't obeying the owner. If it were under control the owner could call it to him or her and the pet would come.

If the owner hasn't time for this obedience training, turn the pet over to a professional. But control over the wild dog must be achieved some way and the only way is through obedience.

When the dog minds, comes when called, and you think that in his mind he acknowledges that you are the boss, keep the leash and collar on him just in case. If he should start running around the house when the doorbell rings, you can get hold of him much easier when he's wearing a leash.

Don't coax him. Use that leash with a sharp upward movement of the hand to tighten the collar, and make him keep quiet and sit down. And don't let him steal one inch when he's told to sit or lie down near you. If he moves put him back where he was told to say. We can't emphasize too much this insistence on *strict* adherence to a command when you are training a nervous telephone barker, especially if the dog has been something of a problem due to misbehavior.

A soft owner never gets control over a wilful dog that slowly is becoming an excessive barker.

That's the sentence we'd like to put in every home where the otherwise lovable and amusing house pet has gotten out of control and has become a chronic barker.

There's no short cut, no bit of magic you can resort to, to

quiet these dogs. They must be brought under control first and then you have some chance of keeping them quiet.

YARD AND KENNEL BARKERS

You use the same routine for pets that bark at everything from a butterfly to a pedestrian. If you have a big fenced yard and let the dog run at will in it, the chances are that someone will come along and tease the pet. Then the barking starts. Or he may just yip his head off when any pedestrian walks along the sidewalk on the other side of the fence. Give most any pet a couple of weeks of this and he is apt to become a nuisance barker. This may be partly due to boredom and partly due to the watch dog instinct. And the very nervous dog is a sure shot to become a nuisance barker under such conditions.

The point that many owners overlook in this wide-open-yard and run-at-will situation is this: if children tease this dog behind a fence, it may not be long before he considers everybody on the other side of the fence an enemy. So anybody coming through the gate is to be barked at and perhaps attacked.

Then you have a perfect example of an uncontrolled barker who may become a biter, largely due the owner's negligence. Big yards for dogs are wonderful. But they also can be the best means of developing barkers.

If you see your dog turning into a yard barker, better take hold of him at once. Put him into training. Make him heed your voice command. But don't expose him to a chance to use his voice. You can't blame a dog for barking at someone who pokes sticks at him through a fence!

Several tricks have been tried to keep a dog from barking too much in a small kennel close to a home. We have such a kennel (small one for a couple of dogs). We never have any trouble with excessive barking due to the fact that the dogs are under control. They are obedience trained. So all we have to do is to speak to them when they get noisy. A few weeks of this training and they catch on to the fact that unnecessary barking can't be done.

MUZZLE TO STOP BARKING?

To resort to a muzzle to stop a house pet from barking seems to us the cruel way to end a fault in a dog. On the other hand, it's possible to use a muzzle purely as a training accessory in curing a dog of excessive barking. We know one trainer who uses it this way: first he gives the untrained, uncontrollable spoiled dog a course in obedience training. Once the dog is under control and obeys a command he finds it will stop its noise making when told to. But in the case of a stubborn, confirmed barker that starts something when it feels it is safe to do so, he catches the offender in the act, scolds it and then puts a muzzle on it.

It's left on the dog for only a few minutes. Just long enough for the animal to get the idea of what discomfort it brings. Then he takes it off but always *hangs it up where the barker can see it.*

If the dog begins to sing later on, the trainer again goes to it, scolds it, reaches for the muzzle which is in plain view of the culprit, and again puts it on the dog.

Even the most stubborn pet soon catches on to this routine. It realizes that when it barks there not only is a scolding due but that uncomfortable thing goes around its mouth.

We can understand why a trainer would use a muzzle in this way. But to strap a muzzle on a pet that's become a nuisance barker due to neglect by the owner and to keep it on the dog for hours is, to us, nothing less than cruel.

Curing the Car Chaser

Dogs that chase cars are not only a problem and a nuisance in any neighborhood, but there also are far too many of them in this country. The car chasers definitely are a factor in causing anti-dog laws in many villages, towns and cities, yet year after year careless and indifferent owners let their pets run the streets to become noisy and much disliked members of the canine population.

The owner of a pet that has become a chronic pursuer of, and barker at, moving automobiles invariably wants to know just one thing: how the dog can be cured of the habit very quickly. To a lesser degree, there is some interest in why dogs like to chase cars. But not much.

Both questions are easy to answer. But eradicating the dangerous and offensive habit of chasing cars takes training, considerable patience, some time and, probably most important, a knowledge of how to conduct the right training and use the firmness required to maintain control over the wayward pet.

Any dog can be cured of chasing automobiles by following a strict routine. Take the dog off the street. That stops the game of car chasing, but obviously doesn't stamp out the habit. But you can't get anywhere in the training routine unless you remove the temptation for the dog to run after an automobile.

The second step is to train the dog in obedience. We know it sounds silly to the owner to talk about training the dog to walk at heel, sit on command, lie down and obey other commands that seemingly have nothing to do with a pet tearing down the street yipping at a car. But the very important point here is to get control over your dog. Control means obedience. It also means that the dog will respect your orders. And, in eradicating a bad habit, it will take control and obedience before you win over the dog. Anyway, every house pet should have the obedience training urgently required by a car chaser that has been running footloose and free.

If you haven't time to train the dog to mind you, you can turn him over to a professional and have him give the dog (and you) lessons in obedience. He will have you rehearse the pet many times to make sure your commands snap and you exact obedience.

We now suppose you have the dog off the street and that he is under control. He minds probably for the first time in his life! You have control over him.

Now comes the further training and test.

Have some member of the family drive the car past you and the dog as you two stand on the lawn, close to the street. You carry in your right hand a short piece of light chain, the kind that is used to put on a dog's collar when he's on the bench in a dog show. That's for throwing purposes.

If the dog moves from your side to run after the car throw that chain at his hind legs. Be sure you aim right. Make a good score on that toss. When the chain strikes his hind legs (it won't hurt him but it will startle him), call his name and get to him as fast as you can. Grab him by the collar and give him a good shaking. Talk to him. Get a grip with both hands on his neck and make him understand he really did wrong.

The reasoning behind this chain routine is this: your dog is stopped in the act of disobeying you and he feels he's punished, but he doesn't know that you did it. He didn't see you toss the chain at his legs. So you have the association built in his mind of running after a car, the "car" did something unpleasant to him and then there you were grabbing him. And don't be too easy on him. When you shake him, do a good job of it.

You may have to repeat this several times. Chronic car chasers, permitted to continue their habit through neglect of the owner, are not easily broken of their favorite sport.

Another system that we have tried is this: do everything in the above outline, including the obedience work, and then finish the lesson from the auto itself. We tried this on a spaniel we once owned immediately after he barked at a car.

We had our neighbor drive us in the front seat of his car. Our equipment consisted of a 25 cent water pistol filled with water and a little cheap perfume. (A tiny bit of ammonia will serve in place of the perfume). In one hand we also had a short piece of chain.

When the dog rushed to the car we gave him a "shot" from the water pistol. That turned him around, startled, and then we leaped from the door and tossed the chain at his hind legs. The dog was shocked and frightened by the way the car had "attacked" him! Then he heard his name called and there was the Boss to see his confusion. We took his collar, shook him a couple of times and put him in the kennel. For the next few hours we went back there and shamed him every 30 minutes or so.

He never forgot that lesson.

This was the only dog we've ever owned that showed the slightest interest in running after a bicycle rider or an auto. Reason? Control and training. Our dogs aren't any smarter than your's. They aren't super-dogs at all. But they mind, are under control, are exercised under supervision, and never run the streets. So they can't become car chasers!

As is the case with many bad habits in dogs, it's so much easier to avoid one than to cure it. And you avoid letting the dog develop a bad habit by proper care and training.

Dogs Must Have Exercise

A normal healthy dog needs daily exercise just as a normal healthy human needs some exercise. In every home the dog gets as much exercise as the owner permits. If the latter won't take their pets for walks obviously the dog can't get very much exercise, unless he's allowed to run wild.

The amount of outdoor exercise required by all dogs can't be measured in terms of time, or blocks or miles covered by the pet and the owner. For example, a shortlegged dog like the popular dachshund gets a lot of exercise when walked just a few blocks. That distance is hardly a warm up for a young setter, pointer, airedale, Labrador retriever, golden, standard poodle or other medium-sized or large-sized breed.

The correct and most pleasant way to give exercise to your dog is to walk with him. You can let him romp off a leash if he's under control, will obey your commands, and there is no danger of cars. If he is not trained he'll have to be walked on a leash. This isn't nearly so much fun for the dog nor for you, which is another good reason for training your dog in obedience.

In hot weather it's not advisable to let the dog exercise much during the heat of the day. Better take him for his walks mornings and evenings when it's cool. Most dogs do not mind cold weather. And those that live in the snow belt can be walked all winter. If you own a smooth coated toy, a Boston terrier or other breed that welcomes a little extra in the way of an overcoat during winter weather, drop into a shop selling dog accessories and buy your pet a sweater or blanket.

If you want to give your dog more exercise than you wish to take during a stroll, teach the pet to retrieve a small dumb bell or other object. Take it along and have your dog make retrieves in a vacant lot or some other spot that is available for this fun.

*An irresistible invitation from a swell pal who wants to go walking.
Dogs of all ages thrive on exercise, although some very active breeds
require more than others.*

Overfeeding and too little exercise can make a dog very
fat. You can't take off this poundage in a hurry. It takes
time because a very fat dog must be brought along slowly to
a point where it can be given even 15 minutes of vigorous
outdoor exercise.

When your faithful old pal gets along in years he neither
needs nor wants a great deal of exercise. Take him walking,
of course. But if he shows signs of tiring, bring him home
and let him curl up for his nap. Some dogs are old at ten
years. Others are pretty peppy at 12. You have to be the judge
of how much or how little outdoor exercise the old dog can
take or wants.

Nothing is so essential to the good looks and skin condition of a dense-coated dog as plenty of brushing and combing. The hair on and behind the ears of a cocker should not be neglected when a comb is used.

Dogs Should Be Well Groomed

Keeping a puppy clean and free of dog odor isn't such a big chore if the owner will follow one or two simple routines. Even a pup that's all or mostly white can be kept neat and clean if you'll use a little elbow grease—after first visiting a shop that sells accessories for grooming dogs of all breeds.

Is it all right to give an eight, ten or twelve weeks old pup a bath? No, it isn't. If you want to scare your puppy out of two weeks growth and possibly make him afraid of a bath the rest of his life just gedunk him in water when he's very young. And (as your veterinarian will tell you) bathing a pup during cold weather isn't smart if you care much for the health of the little fellow.

It's no secret that most American dog owners over-bathe (and over-feed) their pets. Yet it's easy to keep a pup of any size or color very clean without resorting to water and soap.

Here is the formula: go to a dog accessory shop and get a comb and a brush. The clerk will advise you about both if you tell her the breed of dog you have. Then take a look at the dog "toiletries."

These preparations remove dirt (but not the oil from a pup's coat), and the doggy odor. We have kept a Sealyham terrier (nearly all white) clean, free of dirt and objectionable odor an entire winter without giving him a single bath with soap by using these modern preparations that can be purchased in most any store or shop selling dog accessories.

HOW TO GROOM THE PUP

To get the little pup clean put him on a box or table. Placing him on something above the floor is partly for your convenience, but it's also a little psychological trick. The pup is at home on the floor. But place him on a table or box and

51

he's a little awed. That means you can work better and wrestle with him less!

Number one exercise in this routine is a thorough brushing and combing. There is no substitute for this in grooming any dog, of any age or size. The brush and the comb are a must with a capital "M." Brushing and combing take out loose hair, remove most of the dirt and stimulate the dog's skin. Only a lazy and indifferent owner skimps on brushing and combing!

After this exercise you can tackle the odor and dirt that hasn't been removed by brushing and combing. Or maybe there's a stain on the pup's white coat where he's rolled in something.

Here is where those preparations made expressly for cleaning dogs come into play. As we pointed out above, you'll find these on sale in stores and shops selling dog accessories. The liquids usually have a pleasant odor. Some of them contain a cleaning agent (not soap), and an ingredient that serves as a deodorant. The one we use can be sprayed on the dog and then wiped off with an old towel or a wash cloth. And you do not have to use water at all with many of these special dog cleaning preparations.

There also are powders made especially for cleaning puppies or old dogs. These are used much like the liquids. First comes the brushing and combing. Then you dust the powder into the coat of the pup and brush it out. These special powders remove dirt and also kill dog odor.

BAKING SODA AS A CLEANER AND DEODORANT?

The answer is "No." Soda is an alkaline. A veterinarian who is a specialist on skin ailments of dogs says that he is not too sure that making the dog's skin alkaline is a good thing, because a dog's skin, when normal, is slightly on the acid side. Anyway the special toiletries made for dogs are far better than baking soda.

We consider the preparations now available for cleaning dogs without water and soap so easy to use and so good for the dog's skin and coat that for years we have relied on them in keeping our dogs clean without giving them a bath.

GROOMING THE OLDER PUP AND GROWN DOG

If you want to give your dog a bath don't put him in the tub until he's around six months of age. Far more important in basic grooming is the use of brush and comb. Every dog with a dense or long coat should be brushed and combed several times a week. If you don't watch the cocker spaniel or the springer that runs around a good deal, and brush and comb them frequently (especially during the summer in the northern states) they'll pick up burrs which are hard to remove if they aren't taken out of the hair quickly. Then there is the angle of matted hair behind their ears.

All cocker, springer and other spaniel owners should use a brush and comb on their dogs to avoid matted hair, especially behind the ears. When this spot is neglected the hair may get matted so badly that you may have to cut out the patch with scissors.

Another place on dogs with long or dense coats that needs attention is around the feet. Some cockers grow so much long hair around their toes that they look very unkempt and also pick up a lot of dirt to be tracked into the house. Put the pet on a table or box and trim that excess hair away from his feet. The dog will look better and also be neater around the house.

SHEDDING TIME

When older dogs shed in the spring or early summer we find it takes considerable elbow grease to reduce the loose hair problem in the home. In grooming our Labrador retriever when she is losing the undercoat in the spring, we first loosen the hair with our hands by rubbing the dog against the natural growth of hair. Then we finish with a brisk combing and brushing. This routine sometimes has to be repeated several times.

If the weather is mild she gets a warm water bath with lots of massaging of her coat and skin which loosens the dead hair. After the bath and when she is dry we give her a 15 minute combing and brushing. We find this system gets rid of a lot of falling hair quickly.

The first step in giving your dog a bath is to wash his face with a moist wash cloth. Be careful not to get soapy water in his eyes.

Soap and water should be kept out of the ears of your dog, so before the bath starts put a wad of cotton in each ear.

In soaping the dog's coat it's a good idea to start with his head and then work backward, being careful to keep soapy water away from his eyes.

The bath is almost over little cocker, so be patient! The outer ear of the dog may be cleaned with a wash cloth, but no moisture should get into the inner ear.

A thorough rinsing to remove all soap from the dog's coat is necessary. Note how the water is kept out of the dog's face.

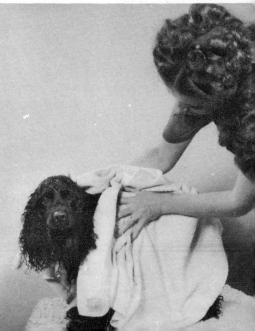

A brisk toweling finishes the bath. When the dog is dry a good brushing and combing puts the final touches on this canine beauty treatment.

SHAMPOOING

Any dog that gets a bath once a month and is brushed and combed frequently should be able to go anywhere in society and be considered as eminently acceptable! Owners who put their pets in the tub for a scrubbing once a week or twice per month are not only treating their dogs badly and doing a lot of unnecessary work, but also contributing toward a possible skin ailment in their pets.

If you're going to shampoo your dog get a mild soap, have the water warm and ease the dog into his bath gently. Better put a wad of cotton in each ear so water and soap won't get into the sensitive inner part of the ears. Start scrubbing the pet around the neck first (especially if you are using a flea soap) and then work backward.

All soap must be rinsed from the skin. Use towels to dry the pet. If the bath is given the dog during cold weather, make sure he's dry before you take him outdoors.

Above all, don't get soap suds in his eyes. Remember how soapy water makes your eyes smart. The dog gets the same re-action from it.

DRY CLEANING YOUR DOG

Some years ago when we first experimented with preparations to clean a dog without soap and the use of water, some of our readers wrote us to ask if a cleaning fluid used to remove grease spots from clothes was all right for dogs!

The answer is "No." A thousand times "No." Those liquid concoctions made for cleaning clothes are NOT usable on dogs.

When you dry clean a dog you must buy a preparation made especially for canines. These you can obtain in any store or shop selling dog accessories.

We find these invaluable in the winter when we do not bathe our dogs. That's right—we never give our dogs a bath during the cold months. Not one. But we do work on them frequently with one of the cleaning preparations made especially for canines. Of late we use a liquid which we buy in a shop selling dog accessories. It has a delightful odor (almost a dog perfume!), kills dog odor and removes dirt. To apply it we take an old wash cloth and dampen it with the liquid. Then we scrub the dog with this. The next step is to rub him vigorously with an old towel. The result is a clean, odorless pet.

GROOMING THE TERRIER BREEDS

There is no use evading the question of how to make the terrier breeds look well by proper grooming; it's not an easy job and you'd better take some lessons from a professional handler at first.

Another thing about barbering terriers like the wire, Scotty, Welsh, Sealyham, Cairn, Kerry blue and others: you won't learn the tricks of correct canine barber work during the first lessons. And if you tackle the barbering business alone don't expect a smooth job at first because canine trimming is much like learning how to cut a human head of hair.

We're not trying to discourage terrier owners from taking lessons in canine barbering. If you have the time take such lessons. Moreover, wiry coated breeds need consistent attention to their coats, if ever a group of dogs did.

When you decide to take up a course in trimming your terrier ask a professional first to give you a lesson and at that time have him explain to you how the various implements required are used. You will need a box on which to stand the dog. And the professional will show you the contrivance he uses for holding a dog while he works, especially around the dog's head. Then there will be such accessories as a steel comb, a good brush, a pair of regular barber scissors, stripping knife and possibly clippers.

Another big help for the beginner is a trimming chart that shows how and where the hair is taken down or left on different parts of the dog. These are available in some dog accessory shops and also in bookstores.

GROOMING SMOOTH COATED BREEDS

The dachshund, pointer, Dalmatian, Boston terrier and similar breeds need little grooming compared to the Scottish terrier, setter, cocker, springer and other breeds with wiry or rather heavy coats. A smooth coated dog in healthy condition needs only a minute or two with a grooming glove or brush and his coat will shine. If you want to get quite technical and really work on a smooth coated dog you can devote some time to the ears. If you examine the ears you'll see just a little longer hair at the edges which can be trimmed. But just brushing or a few licks with a grooming glove is about all you need to do to make those smooth coated dogs look neat.

TRIMMING THE LONG COATED BREEDS

Cocker spaniels, springers, Irish setters, English setters, springer spaniels and others with similar coats have to be brushed, combed and trimmed if they are to present a neat appearance. The average owner either will have to take a lesson or two from a professional handler on how to barber these dogs, or get a trimming chart.

For example, to do a good job on a setter you should strip the hair close on its face and upper throat and also on the top of the head, thin out the hair on the neck and the shoulder, but leave the hair long on the chest and other parts of the body as designated by the chart.

The cocker spaniel also should be stripped down on the face, head and neck, have the hair on some parts of the body thinned out, and get special attention to the feathering on the legs. In other words, a really top notch job of making a cocker spaniel look like something out of the book and as neat and smart as a Beau Brummel among dogs takes a professional touch at first. That means watching a professional do the job first and then taking lessons from him.

But all of us who own dogs with rather heavy or long coats don't need lessons with a brush and comb. What we need is the incentive and desire to do right by our pets and give them the most important grooming routine known—just plain brushing and combing very frequently!

Skin Troubles

Puppies are not so prone to have skin trouble as grown dogs. If you brush and comb the little fellow, feed him correctly and do not use strong deodorants on his skin and coat, it's likely that the first case (if any) of canine skin irritation that you will see is when the pet is grown up. Therefore, all of us who own dogs have to learn at least the basic facts about some of the things that can happen to the coat and skin.

For years we've taken great pleasure in tossing all cases of canine itch, eczema, "hot spots" (red inflamed areas on the dog's skin), and other skin troubles into the lap of a veterinarian. They can have 'em, because the skin trouble problem is too complicated for all of us amateurs. It takes a professional to tell the difference between some irritations that to the untrained eye look almost alike.

Some of the principal facts about skin irritations are these:

1. If your dog develops some red, very inflamed spots on his body, and they cause him to scratch himself a lot, with consequent loss of hair around these areas, don't apply a strong mange remedy. The chances are that the pet hasn't true mange. And don't let your neighbor tell you differently! The trouble is that many owners are inclined to call any skin irritation that causes red, raw or dry spots on the skin "red mange." But true mange is not nearly as common among dogs as stubborn eczema, or another type of skin trouble to be discussed below. That's not just our opinion. That's a fact obtained from veterinarians, some of whom treat hundreds of cases of skin trouble every year.

None of us who own dogs could make a positive, sure diagnosis of true mange without a microscope, the kind that a veterinarian has in his small animal hospital. And here is the reason why: mange is caused by a tiny living parasite which can be seen only through a microscope. The veterinarian pins down a real case of mange by taking a scraping from the dog's skin, putting it under the microscope, and looking for that little "bug."

So if your dog has inflamed areas on his skin, better go easy on those mange remedies until a veterinarian has made his examination.

2. Quite a few skin irritations that come during the summer months when the dog is running around outdoors may be due to vegetation. The pet may pick up a fungus which clings to the skin and inflames it. Some of these cases are anything but pleasant to look at, especially if much of the breast, stomach and other underparts get very red, and the hair falls out. Or a dog may roll on the grass and get similar irritated areas on his back. If it's a bad case, the chances are ten to one that you'll be certain red mange has come—at last. But on the contrary this "fungus itch," "summer itch" or whatever you want to call it is not mange at all. Veterinarians can handle this type of irritation effectively with certain remedies. And if a veterinarian isn't available you can apply patented preparations on sale in shops selling dog accessories. We've seen one case of this "fungus itch" in our dogs. We cleaned it up (after veterinarian made sure of the type of irritation) in about six days.

3. The flea is not to be taken lightly in this business of avoiding or curing cases of skin trouble. Any dog that has fleas is bound to scratch himself a lot. This constant scratching may inflame areas of the skin and these may be the opening wedge for a more serious type of skin trouble. Keep your dog free of fleas if you want to reduce tne chances for possible skin trouble.

ECZEMA

A case of eczema looks awful, may cause hair to fall out and makes a dog miserable. The most recent case we treated on one of our dogs wasn't easy to clean up. The pet had three very moist "hot spots" on the neck and back. They kept getting larger. The hair came out all too easily. And, of course,

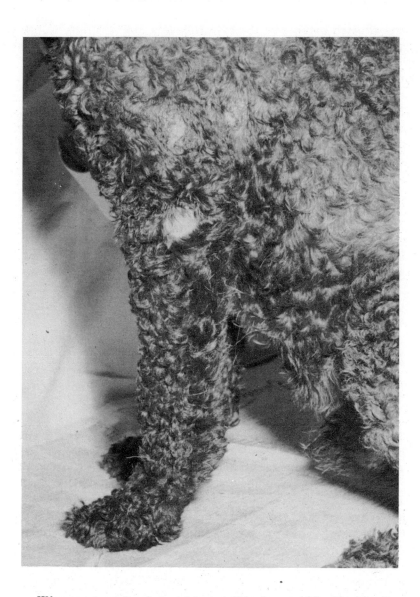

When your pet develops ugly spots like these on his skin, it's time to consult a veterinarian. Ringworm, eczemas and other vexatious types of skin trouble of canines call for diagnosis by a veterinarian so that proper medical treatment will follow. This picture was made in the Jaffray Animal Hospital.

the affected patches of the skin itch so a dog naturally wants to keep after 'em. That makes the inflammation worse.

In a case like this we do not attempt to play a doctor's role. We had the dog checked at a small animal hospital, because some eczemas are due to internal causes, got a soothing lotion from the veterinarian to put on the inflamed areas and, in time, the dog came back to normal. Some of these eczemas are hard to cure. Many are pretty slow in responding to treatment. We consider them very much beyond our amateur rating. Better give 'em to your veterinarian.

RINGWORM

This skin trouble is well named. It's a round sore on the skin of the dog. Fortunately this form of skin trouble is not very common. But it can be communicated to humans, so don't fool with it at home. In our estimation, this is another one that is best handled at first in a small animal hospital.

"ITCHITIS"

If you look in a canine medical dictionary you won't find this word "itchitis," but we can't think of a better one to describe this situation which isn't too uncommon.

A much loved house pet is being given the best of care. The family believes it is feeding it the best way. It's even brushed and combed frequently. Flea killing preparations are used to keep the dog free of these annoying pests.

But the dog scratches itself from morning until night. Examination shows no fleas, no ticks, no lice. Still the dog scratches and far too much hair is coming out. But not a sign of a red inflamed spot on the dog to indicate eczema or other disorder.

What's wrong? In many cases (not all) it's a simple factor in the diet of the dog: not enough fat. The pet is being given cooked horse meat, cooked beef, a high grade prepared food, and possibly a vitamin concentrate, all of which are excellent items. But the animal lacks sufficient fat to produce a fatty acid (stearic) needed for it to be entirely healthy.

We discussed this point with a prominent veterinarian a short time ago. He remarked that until all dog owners realize that dogs need a fair amount of fat in their diets, we're going to see pets with "itchitis" and falling hair. And he added that he was the best lard salesman among veterinarians!

We learned about this fat requirement some years ago. Since then we've discovered that if you want a beautiful shiny coat on a dog, a dog that has a healthy skin and growth of hair, drop some fat in his evening meal.

Don't worry about the pet getting indigestion from eating a little fat. He can handle it all right, especially if it is raw. In fact, it's no trick for a normal pet to digest pure lard. About two tablespoons is enough for a medium sized dog. Suet, bacon drippings or lard will do the trick. Try this for a few weeks and watch the difference in your pet's coat!

There's just one word of caution on this feeding of fat plus the pet's regular meal of prepared food, or whatever you give him. Remember that the feeding of fat may increase your dog's weight.

EXCESSIVE SHEDDING

Dogs that shed hair all winter when they spend most of the time in the house, usually are victims of a sedentary life too close to a radiator, or of rooms kept too warm during the cold months. This is not uncommon among pets that aren't exercised outdoors a great deal during the cold months, or among those that are permitted to sleep in warm rooms. There isn't much you can do about it unless you make the pet sleep in a cool room, and take him outdoors for exercise as much as possible. Otherwise constant exposure to dry heat in the home will make him shed.

If the dog is not getting a fair amount of fat in his diet, remedy that situation and the chances are that he will not offend so much with hair on the rugs and elsewhere in the house.

GETTING RID OF DANDRUFF

When a whitish powder or even flakes appear during the combing and brushing of the dog's coat, the animal has

The object held against the skin of the Chihuahua by this assistant in a small animal hospital doesn't hurt the dog at all. It's a magnifying instrument for the purpose of examining the skin of a dog.

a dandruff condition. We have seen this condition on several of our dogs. Apparently there are many causes of dandruff. In some cases it may be due to the dog being unclean. The pet that stays in a warm house most of the winter and is bathed very frequently may be a candidate for this skin condition. One veterinarian tells us that in some cases this unhealthy skin condition can indicate the presence of parasites.

We notice it in our dogs at the end of the winter, just before they begin to spend much time out of doors in the sun. Your veterinarian can advise you what to do, or you can try this system: first, rub a little coconut oil into the dog's skin. Massage it thoroughly. Wipe off excess oil with a towel. After 24 hours give the dog a bath. When dry rub a little more oil into his skin.

At the same time make sure he is getting enough fat in his diet and brush and comb him twice each day to remove dead hair and stimulate his skin.

How to Control Insects

TICKS

Of all the external parasites that cling to the skin of the dog, the tick is the worst because it's hard to kill and also may move into the house.

We wish every housewife who is devoting part of her time to the care of a companionable affectionate little dog would insist that some member of the family check the pet every few weeks for ticks, and also learn to recognize one when they see it. In that way a dog can be kept free of these pests. And it's really very easy, even in tick infested areas, to keep a dog that never is bothered by either ticks or fleas—if someone treats him with preparations that kill them. Ticks, unfortunately, have been spreading in the United States, so all of us who own dogs should be on guard against them.

If you have never seen a tick you can recognize one by remembering these facts: it's brown, round and flat in shape, and moves slowly. It's a parasite that is very sluggish in action. A flea is small compared to a tick, especially one that has stuck its head into the skin of the dog and filled itself with blood. And a flea is very active. So don't forget tick characteristics—flat, roundish, brown, and slow in movement.

WHERE TICKS ARE FOUND

A house pet may pick up ticks in grass, weed patches or woods. In some cities they have moved into parks, vacant lots and other areas. We find that they seem to have a population cycle. We recall some summers when we had to treat our dog every other week to kill ticks. Then they decreased in numbers. One summer we failed to encounter a single one in the country where we exercise our dogs.

And one more fact about the tick that we want to stress for the housewife: if your dog has ticks, a few may drop off the pet when he's in the house and then multiply indoors. That's not fun for any housewife.

HOW TO KILL TICKS

It's now easier to avoid and kill ticks than ever before, due to the number of splendid preparations made for this purpose. Some contain DDT. Others are made with a factor called rotenone. And there are good tick killers made with still other effective drugs. You can get these in any pet shop or store selling dog accessories.

Moreover, you can make a choice between a powder and a liquid.

If you find a tick or two on your dog and want to give him a treatment to eradicate the pests, better place him on a box or low table covered with newspapers. If you're using a powder, sprinkle it first behind the ears and around his neck, then work back toward his hindquarters. Leave the powder on him, according to directions written on the preparation you're using. Then you'll have to go after his bed and give it a good cleaning. Just one female tick in the dog's bedding can start a new crop!

USING A DIP TO KILL TICKS

We have used both tick killing powders and liquids in our battle against these little parasites. The liquid we have used makes a dip. In other words, the insecticide is mixed with a certain amount of water. One that we've used is mixed one tablespoonful to a quart. For a big dog we make up several gallons and then proceed like this:

The dog is placed in a galvanized tub. If the pet needs a bath we do that job first and rinse her thoroughly. If it's purely a tick killing job we take a big sponge, soak it with the liquid already mixed and put it into her coat from the ears back. For five or even ten minutes we sponge her with the mixture until we're sure every tick or flea has been drenched with it.

Then we tell her to get out of the tub and the job is done. Do not use towels on a dog being treated with a dip. Let the coat dry naturally.

66

The important points to keep in mind in this job of battling ticks are these:

1. If your dog never has had ticks, but you're wondering if they are in your area, either ask your veterinarian about their prevalence or some experienced dog owner near you.
2. Remember that a dog picks up ticks while running through grass and weeds.
3. Better check your dog every week if your live in a tick infested area and your dog runs around outdoors much. To make this check, have the dog lie down on the floor so you can run your fingers over his skin and thus detect the ticks.
4. Check the dog's bedding for ticks.
5. If you should find a tick in the house better get busy with a water soluble solution of DDT around the floor boards, in all cracks and other places where the insects may hide. An electrically operated hand machine which generates a steam spray to force a tick killing solution into spots where ticks may hide has been used successfully.
6. If you have treated your dog for ticks, and you're sure all were killed, don't relax and figure that the job is done for the entire summer! It's possible for the pet to pick up another crop a few days later, if it is exercised in an area where the parasites are found.

HOW TO KILL FLEAS

The common flea not only makes a dog miserable but has a somewhat similar effect upon a conscientious owner who must watch the pet scratch, scratch, scratch.

There is no excuse for any house pet being bothered by fleas, because of the number and effectiveness of powders and liquids available for killing them. The angle about flea infestation that, in our opinion, never has been stressed enough is that the flea can be a factor in worm infestation. It's bad enough to have these insects worry a dog all summer, but when they are hosts in the cycle of some types of worms, it's time to get busy with insecticides.

Any owner who follows directions on using a powder, liquid, or dip, made especially for killing fleas on dogs, can knock 'em out in a hurry. These preparations can be bought in any shop selling all kinds of accessories for dogs.

LICE

Small, gray colored, and repulsive, the louse fools many dog owners because this pest gets a foothold before the owner knows what has happened. Like the tick, it's a bloodsucker. An owner who never has seen a louse on a dog, often can't believe that the dog has a colony of these "unmentionable" little parasites. We recall a springer owner that stopped us on the street one evening when we were walking a dog.

She reported that her dog was scratching a lot, not a flea or tick could be found, and the dog didn't seem to have any kind of skin trouble. Use of a magnifying glass revealed the presence of lice. We found quite a budding colony of 'em near some matted hair behind one ear, and others on the body of the dense coated dog.

If you want to treat the dog at home, get either a powder or liquid made for killing lice. (The ones used for ticks and fleas do the trick).

For applying an insecticide in powder form, better work on the dog in the garage, basement or outdoors. Put him on a table or box covered with papers. Then work the powder into the skin. Use your fingers to rub it in thoroughly. Don't miss a single part of his body. After waiting for a few minutes, to give the powder a chance to do its work, give the dog a bath with a medicated soap—the kind that will kill fleas and lice.

When the dog is dry, use a comb to remove both the dead lice and the nits.

If you give the dog a dip, the combing also is a must after the treatment.

You'll have to give the dog another treatment like this a few days later. Examine his skin carefully, preferably with a magnifying glass. Don't neglect to give his bedding a complete treatment with an insecticide. That's most important.

Pups May Have to be Wormed

There always has been considerable confusion in the minds of dogs owners about the problem of worms in pups and grown dogs. Some owners, unfortunately, think that a pup has to be wormed every other week over a long period. Others believe that just about every illness a pup may develop may be due to some kind of a worm. The result is that many a little dog that should be treated by a veterinarian for distemper or some other ailment is forced to swallow a worm capsule. This sort of home doctoring does more harm than good, because the average drug used against worms can hardly be called mild. In fact, *all worm medicine is necessarily a poison*.

The point to remember about worm infestation of a puppy is this: very likely the person who sold the new dog to you has wormed it at least once and possibly twice. Ask about this when you take possession of the puppy. Although it's true that many puppies do have worms, your veterinarian will tell you that approximately one-half of those that he checks in the small animal hospital may show "negative." In other words, no worms. Moreover, rare is the breeder who doesn't tackle this worm problem before his pups get very old. A heavy infestation of round worms, for example, can kill a puppy. So you can be pretty sure that if you buy a new dog from a responsible breeder he worms his dogs before they are old enough to leave the kennel.

And he also knows that the better a pup is nourished the less damage worms can inflict on the general health of the little dog.

DON'T OVERDOSE THE PUP

Now, it's conceded that worms can undermine a pup's health. But so can too much worm medicine! Too heavy

69

dosing or incorrect amounts of worm medicine can be fatal. As we pointed out above, too many owners blame worms for nearly every indisposition a pup has. We've known of eight or ten weeks old pups being treated with worm medicine at home, when actually the animals were coming down with distemper. That kind of home treatment may kill a pup which already is very ill. We want to repeat that anything strong enough to kill round, tape, hook or whip worms has to be of a poisonous nature. So the caution is: when in doubt, don't give the pup a worm capsule.

WHEN TO WORM YOUR PUP

This is one of the easiest problems to solve by an amateur owner. If you love your new dog, want to do right by him and protect his health you worm him *after* a veterinarian has made an examination of the pup (or grown dog) and says the animal needs a vermifuge.

There's nothing tricky about the actual job of giving a dog some worm medicine. You can do that at home. The tricky and dangerous thing about the worm medicine business is dosing the pup when he doesn't need it, giving the wrong vermifuge for the type of parasite present, and worming a pup too often.

We want to repeat the above word of caution: if you can, put the question of worming in the hands of a veterinarian. If that isn't possible, or if you have a case of round worms to fight (the most common parasite in pups) buy the medicine and follow directions closely.

MOST COMMON TYPES OF WORMS

Dogs usually are bothered by either round, hook, or tape worms. Their presence can be determined by means of a microscopic examination. None of us amateur owners have microscopes and laboratory equipment to make this examination. That's why we ask the veterinarian to get busy and use his to find out if the pup has worms and the kind they are!

It's bad enough for any dog to have to go through life threatened by the above three kinds of parasites. But there's

70

another—the heartworm—that's a serious killer if not caught in time. A blood test reveals this one in a dog.

This makes it obvious that none of us average owners can take a look at a pup or grown dog and just by looking (without the use of laboratory equipment) calmly decide that the animal has this or that kind of a worm and then proceed to administer the correct vermifuge.

THE ROUNDWORMS

This one is the most common in pups and it's also the one that's fairly easy to handle. Pups commonly get roundworms from their mother. This parasite is two or three inches long, whitish in color and round in shape. Symptoms of the presence of round worms are: gums not a healthy red color, but rather pale; bloating after eating; finicky appetite; and possibly a hacking cough. The cough may be caused by the fact that the round worm larvae move around in the body of a pup and may get into the lungs which cause the cough.

A comparatively new worm medicine now handles this type of worm very successfully. As a rule, a breeder will go after round worms in a litter about the time the pups are weaned. That's around the age of six weeks. If the pups are kept long in the kennel they may be given another worming several weeks later.

TAPEWORM

We've never had any trouble with tape worm in a pup, but some of our grown dogs have become infested with this one which usually is rated as the common type among mature canines.

The tapeworm is a flat, long worm that has the shape of a piece of ribbon. Although we have no degree in veterinary medicine and let the business of diagnosing an ailment remain in the veterinarian's hands, we spotted tapeworm in one of our dogs in this way: first we saw fragments or segments of a worm in the dog kennels and also on the hair near the base of the animal's tail. At the same time we noticed that our terrier was off his feed, eyes not too bright, appetite variable but

71

usually ravenous, and generally didn't look right or behave normally.

We took the dog to a small animal hospital, reported our findings, the veterinarian checked the patient, and treated it.

We left the treatment of this dog up to the veterinarian. (There's a fairly new drug available now which is effective and not too toxic). But this point about killing tapeworms is the one you'll run into: your dog will be wormed, but then don't be surprised if the veterinarian asks that you bring the dog back for a check after about four weeks have elapsed. If one head of a worm is left in the dog following the first treatment, the animal will have to have a second treatment.

Here is where the common flea gets into the picture. Never underestimate the effect of fleas on the health of your pet because this little pest is the intermediate host of the tape worm. The rabbit is also a host. So the caution is: keep your dog free of fleas and avoid feeding the viscera of rabbits.

HOOKWORMS

This is a bad one. It has hooks in its mouth with which it attaches itself to the lining of the intestine. In that position it feeds on the blood of the dog and greatly irritates the intestine. You do not need much imagination to figure out what happens to a dog when infested with this worm which drains the strength of the animal. Symptoms of hookworm are pretty much the same as those indicating roundworms except that the dog may have a loose bowel with blood in it. Better let the veterinarian handle this one, but quickly.

WHIPWORM

This is a tough one for the dog and also the veterinarian. It's a small worm, as slim and fine as a sewing needle, and not more than an inch long.

Some of the symptoms are: variable appetite, possible skin irritations, bad coat, diarrhea, and fits.

If your dog has whipworms it's quite likely that not one but several treatments will be necessary, due to the fact that these pesky parasites lodge in a rather inaccesible spot in the dog's body. This one is strictly for the "pros," the veterinarians, to handle. It's a deadly type of worm, one that can't be killed without the help of a veterinarian.

HEART WORM

This one is a bloodstream parasite found principally among southern dogs. But it's also prevalent among some northern dogs, too. Today it's quite common for southern sporting dog fanciers to buy no new dogs without a veterinarian certifying that they're free of heart worm.

If you have worries about this one, better talk to your veterinarian. He'll tell you that the larvae of this worm get into the bloodstream of the dog, in time reach the heart, increase their numbers and, if not treated by a competent veterinarian, will kill the dog.

ERRONEOUS BELIEFS ABOUT WORMS

There are a lot of funny beliefs about worms that continue to be handed down from one owner to another. And none of 'em are true.

For example, milk will not cause worms. Canned dog food will not give worms to a dog of any size or age. One of our readers wrote us about canned dog food plus toasted whole wheat bread she was giving her dog. She had been told that this combination would cause worms in the pet. The answer is that neither rye bread, whole wheat bread, potato bread, white bread, sweet rolls, nor any kind of bread product has anything to do with intestinal parasites. Nor is canned dog food, made with horse meat, beef, fish or other similar products, a factor in producing worms.

Don't let anybody fool you on these points. Just laugh at such beliefs. They're 100 per cent false.

And don't let our neighbor tell you that a heavy feeding of onions will remove worms from a puppy. That's just as false. And you are wasting your money when you dose your dog with garlic with the idea that it will act as a vermifuge.

Give the puppy lots of milk. That nourishing food positively will not cause worms.

Inoculate Against Rabies

Rabies is a serious disease of dogs, foxes, squirrels and all other warm blooded animals.

Your very young puppy doesn't need an inoculation against rabies. But the older dog should have this protection. Ask your veterinarian when he wants to gives this treatment. We've never owned a dog that wasn't inoculated against rabies, although the village in which we live has seen just one case in about 10 years.

The things every dog owner should remember about this disease are these:

1. Rabies has nothing to do with the common fit or convulsion that a pup or older dog may have due to indigestion, worms or other causes. Don't let anybody stampede you with a cry of "mad dog" when a poor pooch has a fit. RABID DOGS do not have such fits. Ask your veterinarian. He'll tell you about fits that dogs may have.

2. When you exercise your dog in a park or around your home, he can't pick up rabies in the course of his walk, unless he meets a rabid animal and is bitten.

Anyone who owns a dog, walks with it, supervises its exercise and does not let it run wild from morning until night has little to worry about rabies because (don't forget) a normal healthy pet must have a contact with an infected dog to contract rabies. On the other hand, if you let your dog run all day, permit it to roam all over the countryside, you are running a possible risk, for these roaming pets are the ones that can encounter a rabid stray.

You never hear of a case of rabies in a kennel. Why? The dogs are confined to certain runs and exercise grounds so they can't have a contact with any kind of a rabid animal unless it's a rat or ground squirrel, which is not a very likely incident.

Beware of Distemper

High on the list of things you must do to guard the health of your new dog is to have him immunized against distemper. Of all the diseases that dogs have, distemper is one of the worst. It's the scourge of young dogs. If you want to compare distemper with an illness that humans are susceptible to, think of this canine disease as a very severe influenza especially deadly to puppies.

Here is where you should talk to your veterinarian. As soon as you have acquired the pup talk to your veterinarian about the best time to have the little fellow take his treatment to prevent distemper. Or, better yet, have him look over the pup and advise you on this subject, check the dog and give you counsel on several health items.

He'll tell you that distemper is infectious, sneaks up on the pup before you may realize what it is, and is nothing to take lightly. It doesn't affect people.

None of us amateurs are qualified to diagnose a case of distemper but you'd better be suspicious and take your dog to a small animal hospital if this happens: your pup, who is ordinarily lively, playful and eats heartily, is a bundle of energy and full of fun, suddenly gets sluggish, refuses to eat, doesn't want to play, and acts as if he just wanted to sleep or lie quiet. Don't hesitate. Let a veterinarian look at him AT ONCE. And if the pup has a little touch of diarrhea in addition to these symptoms, by no means delay getting medical attention.

Many dog fanciers ask us if it's safe to bring a new dog into a home after there has been a case of distemper there. The answer is yes after a reasonable length of time. One veterinarian tells us that the distemper "bug" can't live in a clean well-kept home for long.

A Dog's Teeth Need Some Care

The dog is lucky. He doesn't suffer from toothaches! But that doesn't mean he may go through his life span without any attention to his teeth.

Here are some of the things about canine teeth that all of us should keep in mind:

1. A dog gets two sets of teeth during his life. The first set serves him for only a few months. Then they are replaced by the second or permanent set.

2. A dog's permanent teeth usually are "in" by the time the pup is six or seven months old.

3. A dog with his second and final set of teeth has forty-two.

4. Pups may be upset during teething time (growing of second set). They may show a desire to gnaw anything they can find in the house or in the kennel. Others may have their "bad days" when they are nervous or even irritable. In other words, growing that second set of teeth can affect pups in several different ways.

5. While the pup is developing his second set of teeth his ears may be affected. This is a fact not commonly understood by many inexperienced owners who will write that their collie pup (for example) won't keep his ears up. Or one is up and the other down and what can be done to make this pet look right? This is not an uncommon thing during dentition. A pup may have floppy ears while growing his second set of teeth. But once the tooth ordeal is over the ears usually assume their correct position.

6. During dentition (age three or four months to six or seven months) give the pup a large smooth bone to chew on. Such a bone is an aid to Nature when a pup is going through the cutting process resulting in a new set of teeth. It's well to remember that at this time providing the pup with a big smooth bone is a lot less trouble than

turning him loose in a room to do his chewing on shoes, table legs, chairs, etc. During dentition pups have a desire to chew something, so why tempt him and lead him into a bad habit by giving him chances to chew the furniture?

7. A pup or young dog rarely needs attention to his teeth if he receives the correct diet and gets an occasional smooth bone for chewing purposes. Such a bone acts like a toothbrush in keeping teeth clean. As one veterinarian told us: "an occasional smooth bone is fine for young dogs. Bones for old dogs with teeth worn down, no."

8. Middle aged and old dogs can be bothered with tartar deposits on their teeth. This condition means offensive breath and (if neglected) sore gums. After owning various breeds of dogs of all ages, we're convinced that any owner who doesn't have a veterinarian examine the pet's teeth once a year (after the dog reaches middle age) is courting trouble.

If you talk to your veterinarian he'll tell you that in these days of well balanced dry and canned dog food which most of us buy for our pets we're apt to forget that the pet also needs something that will make him really work his jaws, and use his teeth occasionally. This exercise of teeth against a hard object like a bone stimulates the gums and, in the case of occasional gnawing on smooth bones, cleans the teeth.

So don't forget to give your dog a smooth bone once in a while. We now are making a practice of buying a big round bone with gristle and tendons on it. A chunk like that gives a big dog thirty or forty minutes of real work as it tries to get through to the bone and finally gnaws on the bone itself.

On the other hand some dogs that get too many bones to work on wear out their teeth too quickly. We once made that mistake with a hunting dog. It was a case of overdoing the bone gnawing business. By the time the dog was six it had the teeth of a ten year old canine.

TOOTH EXTRACTIONS

The older the dog, the more necessary for the veterinarian to check its teeth. In some cases it may be necessary to extract a tooth. If the veterinarian says that he has found a tooth that should be extracted, don't worry about the pet suffering from the extraction. Teeth are removed without the pet feeling any pain.

We've had owners ask our advice about treatment for old dogs with bad mouths due to loose teeth and gum infections, and some deliberately keep their pets from small animal hospitals and proper care because they can't bear to think of the pain the dog will suffer in having teeth extracted!

This is a selfish attitude, condemning the dog to unnecessary discomfort, because canine tooth extraction causes the dog no pain. As a rule, the dog is sound asleep due to the benefit of a helpful drug before he's even touched!

So watch your middle aged and old dog's mouth. Have his teeth checked from time to time. And if you want to clean his teeth occasionally, a piece of cotton or small square of cloth with a little table salt or baking soda will serve as a toothbrush and tooth powder.

OFFENSIVE BREATH

Offensive breath, or halitosis, may be due to several things. For example, a quite common cause is just plain bad mouth due to unclean teeth that should have the tartar removed from them. Some dogs seem to have more trouble from tartar deposits on teeth than others.

If your dog has a bad breath, better get his set of "ivory" checked by a veterinarian. He'll look for bad teeth that could be offending, and he'll also check the tartar business. One loose tooth, which will affect the gum, can give a pet a very offensive breath. The veterinarian will remove the loose tooth, you can, if necessary, swab the gums at home with the medicine handed you by the veterinarian and in a short time, if all goes well, the dog's mouth will be greatly improved.

If the mouth of the pet is all right, your veterinarian will look for other causes of bad breath. This is a situation that is not for us amateurs and our home remedies. It's up to a graduate veterinarian to take over and make the correct diagnosis, and suggest treatment.

Eye Irritations

The longer you own dogs, the more you marvel at the way they go through life with comparatively few eye troubles. If your pet's eyes seem to be irritated from a known cause such as riding with his head out of a car window (a bad habit in any breed!) you treat them with the same simple medicines that you use for minor human eye irritations, such as boric acid or Murine.

If there is a combination pet and hunting dog in the family it may be advisable to put a couple of drops of Murine in the animal's eyes to soothe them and relieve the irritation usually due to dirt and pollen after the dog has been hunting.

But if an owner has reason to think that the pet has some serious eye trouble, better forget the home doctoring business and let a veterinarian prescribe the treatment. The eye is too important and intricate an organ for treatment by amateurs.

Care of the Pup's Ears

The average pup doesn't need any particular attention to his ears unless he gets into an accident causing injury to an ear, or is a representative of a breed requiring an ear trim. The Doberman Pinscher, Great Dane and other breeds (including the popular boxer) bow to the dictates of canine fashion and have their ears trimmed, which makes it rather tough for both dogs and owners.

This is something to be handled by a professional active in the breed you own. Or a veterinarian. However, some veterinarians will not do any ear trimming.

After the pup has developed into a grown dog he will have to have some attention to his ears to keep them as clean as possible and thus prevent (if possible) infections in the inner canal. We've never owned a dog that didn't have to get his ears checked by a veterinarian from time to time, and most of them required, at one time or another, a thorough cleaning. This attention prevented in two instances cases of severe inflammation of the inner ear canals.

We doubt if there is any one angle of dog care so commonly neglected by a majority of dog owners as proper attention to the pet's ears. Dirt accumulates in ears. Dead hair is a contributing factor. Sometimes small seeds from weeds and grass are a factor. Then there is a little mite that likes to lodge in a dog's ears.

When you get an accumulation of foreign matter in the canine ear (usually due to owner's neglect) it's only reasonable to expect that there will be a resultant irritation. However, some breeds seem to be more susceptible than others when it comes to ear irritations. We've had to have a veterinarian watch ears closely in spaniels, a wire haired fox terrier, setters and retrievers that do considerable water retrieving. One setter gave us the most trouble, for despite constant care, she developed a "bad ear" with the inner canal becoming inflamed on the slightest provocation.

THE CLEANING JOB

To clean the ears of your dog remove all the dead hair from the outer ear first. If you want to clean the inside of the outer ear with a moist cloth, all right. But don't get soap and water deep down in the ear. And don't probe deeply into the pet's inner ear. To play it safe clean only as far as you can see. For this work you can use a swab dipped in a little alcohol.

When it comes to going down deep in a dog's ear, better give that job to a veterinarian. He has a trick light that enables him to see the inner ear plainly, for on the tiny light is a magnifying glass.

EAR "CANKER"

If your dog scratches his ears constantly, shakes his head a good deal, and tries to rub his ear on the rug, meantime groaning as if in pain, don't run for the warm olive oil for treatment of this pet. Instead, take him to a small animal hospital right away because the chances are the dog has painful inflammation of the inner ear. This trouble commonly is called "ear canker." That isn't the name the veterinarian gives it. But it's the common name used by many dog owners.

The best advice on what to do for a pup with such an infection is: take him to your veterinarian at once. If no veterinarian is available the next best thing is to try to buy one of the several patented preparations sold in pet shops for ear infections.

We never dilly-dally with one of these ear cases. Our dogs go to a small animal hospital at the first sign of trouble. We want the veterinarian to flash on his little light, see the condition of the inner ear canal, possibly take a sample of the "stuff" down there, look at it under a microscope, clean the ear properly and apply medicine. Then we continue the treatment at home with the remedy given us by the veterinarian.

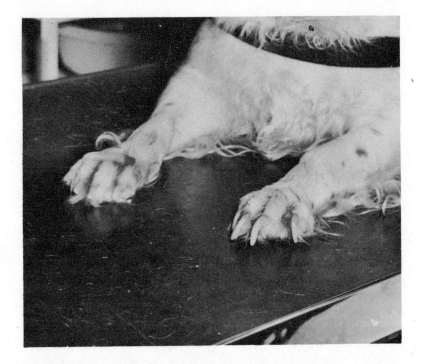

The nails of house dogs often require attention because they grow too long. Note the length of the nails on this dog's left paw. Nails on his other front paw have just been clipped by a veterinarian.

Care of the Dog's Nails

You won't have to worry about care of a puppy's nails. Nature takes care of the little fellow. But after he has grown up he may need a nail trim. The reason is this: any mature dog that doesn't get a lot of running around and outdoor exercise won't have a chance to wear down his nails. The result is that they get too long. This calls for a little work by the owner.

If you don't file or cut the pet's nails he may get sore paws. Some neglected pets may grow nails so long that they begin to curl under. Naturally that's an uncomfortable situation for any dog.

WHAT TO DO

You can give your dog a pedicure in two ways: use either a file made expressly for canine nails, or drop into a shop selling dog accessories and buy a nail clipper. We might add that there's a third way (at first): ask a professional handler or veterinarian to give the dog a pedicure while you watch the routine.

Very likely the most difficult part of treating the pet's long nails is making him stand still if he's not trained in obedience. If you are going to do the job yourself put the dog on a big box or table. In that position you can control him better. If he won't stand still have some member of the family hold him.

In using a nail clipper be very careful that you do not take off too much nail. That will hurt the dog. Better to snip off just a little of the nail end. This is an important point to remember. Don't cut the nail back too far.

In giving a pet adequate nail care all of us must remember that most companion dogs do not run enough to keep their nails at the right length, so most owners will have to lend a hand in this angle of proper grooming.

First Aid for Dogs

TREATING A CUT

If the dog suffers a minor injury as, for example, cutting his foot, or a small gash in his skin, clean it with a little soap and warm water, put some boric acid on it and the chances are it will heal. A long and rather deep cut on a pad we have treated by a veterinarian so it will stay bandaged for several days. Then the dog keeps it clean by licking.

A serious wound that's bleeding profusely, is not for us amateurs. Better call the veterinarian to come on the hop, skip, and jump, while you hold a small cloth or chunk of cotton against it to reduce the bleeding.

WOUNDS FROM DOG FIGHTS

Severe wounds that are either long, or deep, or both, often have to be stitched up, so better get the veterinarian to do the job as quickly as possible. Until he comes, about all you can do is to slow down the bleeding. And don't be surprised if the dog snarls and even trys to nip you when you apply first aid. Many dogs in pain will bite. That's why it is better to leave a dog alone, if the situation permits it, rather than try to do too much before the veterinarian arrives.

AUTOMOBILE ACCIDENTS

If we lived in a community where our dog constantly faced the hazard of being struck by a car, we'd ask the veterinarian for instructions on what to do when such an accident happens because it's a touchy business. A serious accident may involve broken bones, or internal injury or both.

The most heart breaking part of a street accident due to an automobile, aside from the worry and fear caused the owner, can come when the latter rushes into the street to help the poor dog. The dog is down, obviously in great pain. Someone touches it, or tries to pick it up and it bites.

So many owners can't understand this. But the dog may be so dazed, so shocked and in such pain, that this reaction occurs without the animal knowing clearly what it is doing. So better be careful during those first few moments after the dog has been struck by a car. You'll have to get the poor animal off the street. That's the first thing to do. But take it easy and don't move him any more than you have to.

Then call your veterinarian to come at once.

If the dog gets up and walks into the yard, but limps badly, you can suspect a broken bone. Again this is a situation for the small animal hospital.

We wouldn't worry nearly so much about a limp and a possible broken bone, as the chance of internal injury. Watch the animal closely during the hours following his being struck by a car. An internal injury may not show until later. Keep the dog quiet during that time. And if you want to play it safe, have the dog kept under observation by a veterinarian until he says it's okay.

FOREIGN OBJECTS IN THE MOUTH

One day one of our dogs began to work her tongue frantically. She rolled it around inside and outside of her mouth. Then she began to paw at her mouth. When not doing this she coughed and gagged. The obvious deduction was that there was something wrong with her mouth or throat.

It took two of us to examine her mouth thoroughly. While she was sitting down and her mouth held open, we used our fingers to get under her tongue, examine the area next to her teeth, and finally the roof of her mouth and upper throat area.

This exploration discovered the cause of her discomfort. A small flat piece of bone was lodged against the roof of her mouth well back toward her throat. It was pressed against the flesh as if it had been put there with great pressure.

We removed it by lifting it up with a small pair of tweezers, and the trouble was over.

If your pet displays some of the above described symptoms of discomfort, examine its mouth and throat at once. But don't use anything to probe the throat. If you see something you can't handle, get the dog to a veterinarian at once.

HYSTERIA FROM THUNDERSTORMS

Many dogs are scared to death of those high-powered electrical storms that bring tremendous crashes of thunder. We once owned a springer spaniel that loved to hunt, enjoyed the booming of shotguns and was happiest when several guns were booming behind him while the pheasants dropped, yet was very frightened of thunder storms. This dog would try to get into a closet, under a bed or into some other "safe" spot, when a storm was in the offing.

It's not uncommon for some pets to go into hysterics during a bad storm. They may have fits that scare their owners no end.

The kindest thing you can do for your nervous, highstrung dog is to tell the veterinarian about this situation and he will give you some medicine that will act as a sedative. Or he may hand you something that will make the pet sleep during most of the time that the noise prevails.

Firecrackers, cap pistols and other noises on the Fourth of July often have the same effect on dogs as severe thunder storms. Proper care of your pet is the same as above. Ask your veterinarian to prescribe. It's the thoughtful thing to do for your pet. Why have him suffer when a pill or capsule or two will ease him through a bad time?

FIRST AID IN POISONING

There is the chance (especially in cities) that a dog will accidentally pick up food that is poisonous and distributed to kill rats. This is apt to be either phosphorus, often put in some patented rat killing mixtures, strychnine or arsenic. Then there can be the possibility that some cruel and very low member of the human race will deliberately try to poison a dog in some neighborhood. Therefore, it behooves every owner to keep in mind just one or two things about poisoning. We would list those items in this order:

1. Learn to recognize poison symptoms, or at least be suspicious of certain signs that indicate the possibility of poison.
2. Apply first aid at once.
3. Call the veterinarian.

The big job for the owner is to do something quickly if poison is suspected. Get busy with first aid.

SYMPTOMS OF POISONING

If you love your dog don't fail to keep the following symptoms or signs of poisoning in mind:

You may suspect the condition if your dog comes in from the outdoors and gets so sick that it collapses, becomes very ill, or jerks and twitches and trembles. Of course, different poisons, from arsenic to those new weed killing agents, have different symptoms. But remember those just mentioned above and also severe vomiting and diarrhea, accompanied by rapid breathing and trembling.

Go into action at once if your dog shows some of these symptoms. Call the veterinarian at once and then give first aid.

The important thing is to empty the dog's stomach *at once* so that he can't absorb more of the poison.

To do this put a little salt on the back of his tongue. Or grab the baking soda and mix some soda and *warm* water and pour it down his throat. That will act as an emetic.

After the dog throws up, give him another glass of it. If you have milk handy you can force some of that down his throat. Remember, you've got to get everything out of the dog's stomach. Then the veterinarian will take over.

CARSICKNESS

Many pups get sick when taken on their first automobile ride. The majority get over it and learn to love automobile riding. Some, however, never seem to be at ease in a moving automobile. Fortunately these are in the minority. Sometimes it helps the nervous, highstrung dog that becomes ill on an auto ride, to get a sedative. But we've never heard of a magic quick cure for car sickness among canines. If your pet is a real problem, better talk to the veterinarian about it. Here again a sedative (prescribed by the veterinarian) may be a definite help.

CARE OF A DOG WITH A FIT

The important thing for every dog owner to remember about a fit is this: it's a warning that something is wrong with the pet. He's sick and the fit is a symptom, not a disease.

Here are the things you should do at once:
1. Have someone in the family call the veterinarian.
2. Try and get the pup to a spot where he can't hurt himself.
3. If he has a fit on the street, throw something over him if you can and stay near him until he's over the fit. Don't let anybody panic you with a cry of "Mad Dog." A fit is not a symptom of rabies.

We admit that few things scare us more in our dog experiences than when one of our dogs has a fit or convulsion. The way the pet falls over on his side, foams at the mouth and works his legs is enough to frighten anybody. And if the poor animal tears around a room and knocks over lamps and furniture, it's even worse.

After the animal has returned to normal you should have your veterinarian either call for him and take him to the small animal hospital for an examination, or drive the dog to the hospital. Don't delay on this routine. Do it at once.

Remember that a fit is a symptom, a warning. There are a number of causes. A pup that has eaten unwisely may have a fit. Worms may cause a fit.

The important thing to remember about a fit is this: don't try home remedies after the pup is back to normal. It takes the professional knowledge of a veterinarian to find out what caused the fit and treat the cause.

Giving Medicine to a Dog

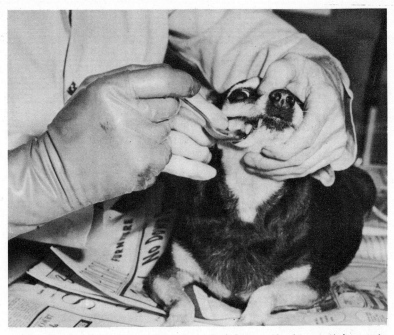

A veterinarian shows how he administers liquid medicine. An assistant holds mouth of dog with left hand while with right he forms opening in the cheek of the patient. Into this "pocket" the veterinarian pours the medicine.

GIVING LIQUID MEDICINE

Have the dog sit down. Take hold of the corner of his mouth and pull it out rather wide. Then quickly put the liquid into this "pocket" and lift his head.

HOW TO GIVE A DOG A PILL

Open the dog's mouth very wide with both hands. Hold the capsule or pill in the right. When the mouth is opened as wide as you can get it, drop the capsule way back on the base of the tongue, close his mouth, hold it closed and tilt his head up. Stroke his throat with the palm of your hand and, when you see him gulp, it's a safe bet the capsule or pill is down.

When Should You Call the Veterinarian?

If our dogs could talk, caring for them and treating their ailments would be so much easier. We can describe our own symptoms when we're ill. The physician thus gets much help in making a diagnosis. But our dogs can't tell us what hurts when they get sick. That makes it difficult for you and me and also for the veterinarian. And, unfortunately, far too many owners delay in asking a veterinarian to check their sick pets.

We've found, in years of dog ownership, that calling for a veterinarian's help when we're in doubt about an illness in one of our pets, is not only smart and more economical, but also the kindest thing we can do for them.

So we suggest that you consult a veterinarian about your dog when:

1. Your puppy loses his pep, acts anything but normal, looks and acts sluggish, has no appetite and instead of wanting to play wants to sleep.

2. You want to find out about immunizing the pup against distemper.

3. The pup has a fit. Better have the veterinarian check your dog at once because a fit, also, is a symptom, a signal that something is wrong.

4. You think your pup has worms, but you are not sure.

5. You see a small swelling on an unspayed female dog, especially if it's on the breast or other place on the underparts of the animal.

6. You want correct information about rabies and how easily a grown pet can be immunized. Don't listen to all the stories and erroneous statements about this disease that you may hear from misinformed persons.

7. Your mature or old dog shows that he has a tough time

chewing hard foods. Some old dogs have tooth troubles that only a veterinarian can treat.

8. Your unspayed female which hasn't been bred, and therefore can't be expecting a litter of puppies, shows signs that she thinks she's going to have a family. These signs may even include a desire to watch over some object as if it were a puppy. There may also be changes in her appearance. This condition is called false pregnancy. You need a veterinarian's help for this condition.

9. When the pup or grown dog has diarrhea for twenty-four to thirty-six hours. That's a symptom. It's imperative to find the cause.

10. When your pet has been struck by a car and you're not sure how serious its injuries are.

11. The dog has a severe ear infection causing it great pain.

12. The pet drops to the floor, can't get up and then has trouble with its legs after it begins to get normal. Don't forget that dogs may develop a serious form of heart trouble.

These and other medical problems that may develop in dog ownership are not for us amateurs. They are for veterinarians.

ACKNOWLEDGMENT

It is a pleasure to thank and acknowledge my indebtedness to several friends in the field of veterinary medicine who have aided in the production of this simple guide on dog care and training. I am deeply grateful to Robert Glover, D.V.M., Evanston, Illinois, for reading and correcting parts of the material on dog care, and for his general counsel on dog health and diseases; to my old friend and canine counselor John Jaffray, D.V.M., Chicago, who helped me with advice and some of the photographic details of the book; to Andrew Merrick, D.V.M., Brookfield, Illinois, whose educational discussions of canine skin troubles and nutrition have been invaluable to me in assembling the material in this book. Also, I wish to thank Mr. R. C. Klussendorf, Assistant Executive Secretary of the American Veterinary Association, for his counsel on several sections of the book.

Bob Becker